The Lily
and the Lion

Royal France

Great Britain

CROYDON COLLEGE

LEARNING RESOURCES
FAIRFIELD, CROYDON CR9 1DX
0181 760 5843

This book is due for return on or before the last date shown below

20/11/08		

181 97

The Rise and Fall of Empires

The Lily and the Lion

Royal France

Great Britain

Philip Mansel
Royal France

Robin W. Winks
Great Britain

Preface by Peter Stansky
Professor of History
Stanford University

CASSELL
LONDON

CASSELL LTD.
35 Red Lion Square, London WC1R 4SG
and at Sydney, Auckland, Toronto, Johannesburg,
an affiliate of
Macmillan Publishing Co., Inc.,
New York.

First published in Great Britain 1981

ISBN 0 304 30761 0

Printed in Italy.

Authors: Philip Mansel, Robin W. Winks
Picture Researcher: Janet Adams

Consultants:
  Royal France: Abigail Mellen
  Great Britain: Severin Hochberg

Design Implementation: Designworks

Rizzoli Editore

Authors of the Italian Edition
  Introduction: Professor Ovidio Dallera
  Royal France: Dr. Flavio Conti
  Great Britain: Professor Ugo Basso
  Maps: Gian Franco Leonardi
Idea and Realization: Harry C. Lindinger
Graphic Design: Gerry Valsecchi
General Editorial Supervisor: Ovidio Dallera

Contents

Preface

The two greatest modern empires of the West have undoubtedly been those of France and Great Britain. Both the French and the British started their imperial adventures through the suppression of contiguous territories, the French by molding the various provinces of France into what could be loosely called a nation and the English by gaining control of Wales, Scotland, and Ireland. In time the two came to extend their authority far beyond Europe. The effect of Britain's influence was most conspicuous in the Western Hemisphere. Through much of the nineteenth century the British were the dominant economic power in South America, with major investments in Argentina (railways), Brazil (government bonds), Mexico (oil), Chile (nitrates), and Uruguay (beef products). In North America, Britain was the formal possessor of Canada and played an active role in the economic development of the United States, especially in the financing of railroads. France, too, established a sphere of influence across the Atlantic, most noticeably in Louisiana and Quebec. The period of French ascendency in North America was relatively brief, so its imprint was more keenly felt in culture than in politics, but the separatist movement in Canada today reminds us of the enduring impact of the French legacy in America.

It was in the eighteenth century that France and Britain battled to determine which would emerge as the greatest imperial state of the modern period. France, in terms of wealth, land mass, and armies, initially appeared to have the edge. Britain, however, with its ever more numerous technological achievements, its growing navy, and its more sophisticated commercial and financial operations, ultimately claimed the honor as the result of wars fought against France in Europe, America, and India. Nevertheless, the British triumph over the French in the American colonies soured when the Americans, no longer in need of British protection, chose to declare themselves independent of the mother country. This action was unilateral, without the mutual agreement that has, in the face of necessity, characterized the attainment of complete or virtual independence by the member countries of the British Commonwealth and almost all other parts of the British Empire in this century.

American independence had profound effects upon the development of both the British and the French empires. For the British it meant a turning away from an empire of settlement toward an empire of control; the most brilliant jewel in the British monarch's diadem was to become the great subcontinent of India. For the French, financial aid to the American rebels proved crucial in bringing about the downfall of the monarchy through the Revolution; there followed the establishment of a republic and the proclamation of Napoleon's empire.

A hundred years of warfare between France and Britain ended at the battle of Waterloo in 1815, with Britain clearly the dominant imperial power of the nineteenth century—master of one quarter of the world's territory and ruler of one fifth of the earth's population. Toward the end of the century, its position was seriously challenged by the colonial activities of a number of European nations—most notably France, Belgium, and Germany—in the "scramble for Africa." (The Dutch had earlier established themselves in Africa.) The colonial legacy remains a potent influence in African life to this day, each African nation revealing the stamp of the European country that ruled it. It is, of course, a matter of debate how beneficial that legacy is, or if it was indeed beneficial at all.

The differing forms of dominance exercised by France and Britain are seen clearly in the contrasting colonial experiences of Egypt. The French presence there had been brief; it was the British who came to rule the nation. Yet Egyptian culture, to the extent that it was affected by the European world, owes considerably more to the French than to the British. The French were much more concerned than the British about exporting their civilization and somewhat more willing to incorporate the conquered society into an idea of a Greater France. Colonial peoples in the British Empire had little voice in the decisions made in their own territories. In institutional terms, however, Britain profoundly affected the development of the territories it occupied.

In their attempts to serve the aims of God, Glory, and Gold, French and British colonizers engaged in pursuits both laudable and tawdry, pursuits that brought forth heroism as well as despicable behavior. Now largely vanished, the empires of the French and British provide a revealing study of how much can be achieved—and how much sacrificed—in the name of progress.

PETER STANSKY
Professor of History
Stanford University

Royal France

France was the center of two sorts of empires: territorial empires, such as those of Charlemagne and Napoleon, and cultural empires, such as those of the Middle Ages and the seventeenth and eighteenth centuries, when the French language and French civilization dominated European culture. And yet, remarkably, the nation that had by far the largest population of any state in Europe until the rise of Russia in the eighteenth century never managed to dominate the Continent militarily for long periods of time. Centuries of wars, rebellions, and miracles—and the repeated efforts of some of the greatest kings, minis-

ters, and generals Europe has ever known—were needed to mold a country chronically weakened by provincial separatism into a unified kingdom.

The region in which royal France grew and flourished—the varied territory between the Atlantic, the Pyrenees, the Mediterranean, the Alps, and the Rhine—had been a prosperous province of the Roman Empire called Gaul. But as the military might and economic wealth of the empire collapsed, Germanic peoples from beyond the Rhine crossed the frontier and settled in Gaul, a far richer and more attractive land than that of their ancestors. During the late fifth century A.D., the Franks—the Germanic

tribe that gave its name to France—arrived in northeastern Gaul. Under Clovis, Frankish king from 481 to 511, they soon became the dominant power in the region.

Clovis, who in 498 converted to Christianity, first established the special relationship between the French monarchy and the Church, a relationship that was to prove highly profitable for both institutions through the centuries. In return for the sanctity and spiritual authority that the Church lent the monarchy, the latter gave the Church protection and numerous benefits. Clovis' dynasty, the Merovingians, founded many of the greatest French monasteries,

Preceding page, the profile of Louis XIV, from a coin minted in 1696. The Latin inscription ("Louis XIV, by the grace of God king of France and Navarre") recalls the origins of the Bourbon monarchs, who were kings of Navarre before becoming sovereigns of France in 1589. Under Louis XIV royal France enjoyed cultural supremacy in Europe and established the pattern for absolute monarchy.

Above, the valley of Oisans, in Dauphiné. After this Alpine province was ceded to France in the fourteenth century, the king's eldest son was given the title of dauphin.

such as Saint-Denis and Saint Martin de Tours. Not only spiritual centers, the monasteries also promoted economic activity, by the fairs held on the feast days of their patron saints, and served as sanctuaries of scholarship.

Although created by the barbarian Merovingian dynasty, the kingdom of the Franks never completely lost touch with its Roman heritage as did, for example, the kingdoms of the Anglo-Saxons. To begin with, the Franks were few in number compared to the mass of Latin-speaking peasants; even after Latin had become a dead language, the new French language was much more Latin- than Germanic-derived. In

addition, the traditional economy of villas and towns—a legacy of Roman rule—remained essentially unchanged until the collapse of Mediterranean trade in the eighth century. And Clovis was not only king of the Franks but also an honorary Roman consul—an appointment conferred by the Roman emperor in Constantinople, who was happy to have this counter-weight to the Arian Christian barbarians ruling Spain and Italy.

The first Merovingian kings were successful war-lords and extremely powerful rulers. Taxes on trade and the income from the huge estates formerly owned by the Roman emperors gave the Merovingians a

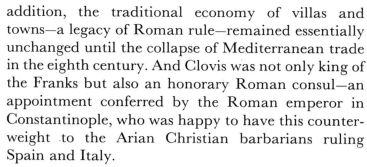

Right, the fertile countryside of the Île-de-France, the province incorporating Paris. Through much of France's early history the possession of this vital area enabled the kings of France to hold their own against extremely powerful vassals. Below, the Canal du Midi, in Languedoc. This area of southern France between the Rhône and Garonne rivers had its own language, customs, interests, and dynasties, all different from those in the north. It became part of the royal French domain only after the thirteenth-century crusade against the Albigenses.

Left, a plateau in the Massif Central region. France, a land of great natural diversity, was shaped into a united kingdom through the relentless efforts of its monarchs. Right, a field in the Île-de-France. These plains of the Paris basin have long been one of France's chief sources of wheat.

Above, the Phare de Creac'h, a lighthouse on the Île d'Ouessant, off the coast of Brittany. Below, the white cliffs of Aval, near Étretat in Normandy. Right, the fertile fields of the Loire Valley near Chinon, in Touraine.

firm financial base. From this position of strength, these monarchs were able to perform two essential functions of French kingship: the assertion of royal authority and the enforcement of the rule of law. (Frankish law had begun to absorb elements of Roman law as early as the sixth century, and Clovis had issued in 506 a famous collection of laws known as the Lex Salica.) A chronicler gives a vivid picture of Dagobert I, one of Clovis' ablest successors, visiting various provinces in the company of his warriors to ensure that justice was impartially meted out to all.

After Dagobert's death in 639, however, the fi-nances of the monarchy began to decline. Trade dwindled, and the kings gave away their estates with thoughtless abandon, particularly to the monasteries. (It was during this period that Saint-Denis, the traditional burial place of French monarchs, became one of the richest monasteries in Europe.) Furthermore, the Merovingian custom of dividing the realm among the king's sons weakened royal authority and gave rise to endless feuds and civil wars.

In 639 the crown passed to the first of the Rois Fainéants, "Do-nothing Kings." These increasingly helpless and pathetic figures were distinguished only by the length of their hair—the emblem of royal

Above, the Rhône near Arles in Provence.

Below, a river valley in south-western France.

power among the Merovingians. Finally, in 751, a member of the prestigious Carolingian family, which had long provided Mayors of the Palace (chief administrators) under the Merovingian dynasty, ascended the throne with the blessing of Pope Zacharias. The pontiff, who needed a strong ally to help him in Italy, crossed the Alps to anoint the new king, Pepin I. Zacharias recognized that the real basis of royal authority was military force, writing that the last Merovingian was shaved, deposed, and shut up in a monastery "because he was not useful." But although the Carolingians had replaced the Merovingians, the nature of the French monarchy as the property of a royal dynasty remained unaltered.

The Carolingian kings brought the monarchy their huge estates in the northeast, where their capital of Aachen (Aix-la-Chapelle) was located, and the prestige of their innumerable victories over the Arabs, the Saxons, and the Slavs. They saw themselves not only as heirs to the anointed kings of the Old Testament—to whom they were regularly compared—but also as successors to the Roman emperors. On Christmas Day 800 the most famous of the Carolingians, Charlemagne, was crowned Emperor of the Romans in St. Peter's Basilica at Rome by the pope himself. Before his death in 814, Charlemagne had extended Frank-

Above, a relief on the tomb of the Merovingian king Dagobert I (reigned 629–639). The Merovingian dynasty soon lost effective power to the Carolingians, who were originally Mayors of the Palace (chief administrators) but later deposed their masters and became kings themselves. Below, a medieval miniature representing the battle of Tours (also called the battle of Poitiers), fought in 732. With this decisive victory under Charles Martel, the Franks blocked Arab expansion into western Europe.

ish rule to northern Italy, Catalonia, and all western Europe up to the Elbe River. Like the Merovingians, however, the Carolingians did not have a fixed order of succession and divided their realm among their adult male relations. As a result, Burgundy, Italy, and the lands east of the Rhine soon split off from the West Frankish kingdom, today known as France.

The Carolingian kings in France grew weaker as a result of their incessant civil wars and the reckless gifts of royal estates they made to their followers. In this way the basis of royal power—the king as a successful warlord able to reward his followers—was inexorably eroded. Moreover, during the ninth century, France became a society of peasants dominated by landowners, who were beginning to form a class of hereditary nobles. These landowners inherited their estates, rather than receiving them from the king, in return for their services as royal officials or soldiers. This social organization was not to change in essence until the seventeenth century.

Peasants were allowed to work on the nobles' estates in return for the goods and services they provided. The nobles, for their part, were expected to protect the peasants, just as the king was expected to protect the nobles. The foundation of French society for the next eight hundred years—until the rise of the absolute monarchy—is summed up in a decree of Charlemagne: "Concerning ordinary folk, let each man so control his dependants that they shall the better obey and accept the imperial [or royal] orders and decrees." French society was a hierarchy of authority whose continued existence was guaranteed by

This page, seven kings of the Carolingian dynasty, which ruled France from 751 to 987. Clockwise from above: a miniature from a fourteenth-century manuscript depicting a conspiracy against Louis the Pious (814–840); the coronation of Rudolf, the duke of Burgundy (923–936); the assumption of power by Charles the Bald (840–877); Louis the Sluggard, the last Carolingian king of France (986–987); Louis IV (936–954); and Lothair (954–986). Near right, Charles the Fat (884–887).

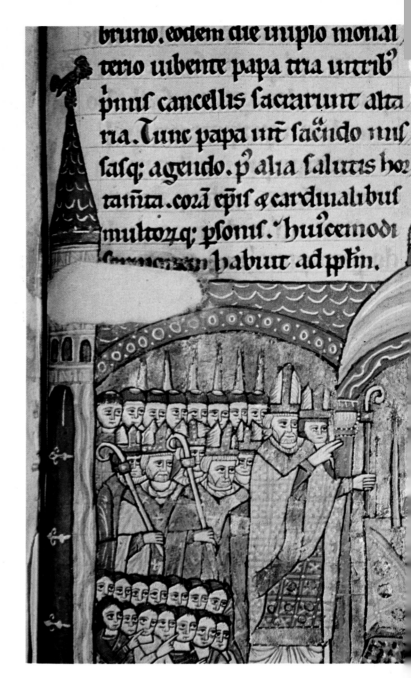

the power of the king and particularly by his ability to control the nobles.

After 850 the Carolingian monarchs were increasingly threatened by Norman (Viking) marauders, who would appear without warning on the Atlantic coast, row up the rivers, pillage, and then set out to sea—usually before the Frankish cavalry had time to assemble to offer resistance. Some Franks, however, fought the Normans and won. Robert the Strong, for example, the count of Anjou, managed to inflict a shattering defeat on the "invincible" Normans in 866 at Brissarthe, though he himself lost his life on the battlefield.

Inevitably there was increasing friction between the realm's powerful warlords and the Carolingian monarchs, who ignominiously bought off the Normans in 911 with a grant of the extensive northern province that became known as Normandy. The Carolingians in time grew too poor to inspire confidence among their subjects or to win followers by the judicious distribution of rewards. After the death of Louis the Sluggard, a descendant of Robert the Strong was selected *rex Francorum* (king of the Franks) by an assembly of nobles in 987. Known as Hugh Capet—from the *cappa,* or ecclesiastical hood, that he usually wore—he founded a dynasty that lasted until the First Republic, which in 1793 guillotined one "citizen Capet," formerly King Louis XVI of France.

The title of rex Francorum, which had been borne by Clovis and Charlemagne, carried immense prestige. But within Hugh Capet's kingdom, which consisted of the western two thirds of modern France, the monarch's authority was little more than nominal. Only the hereditary possessions of the Capet family—

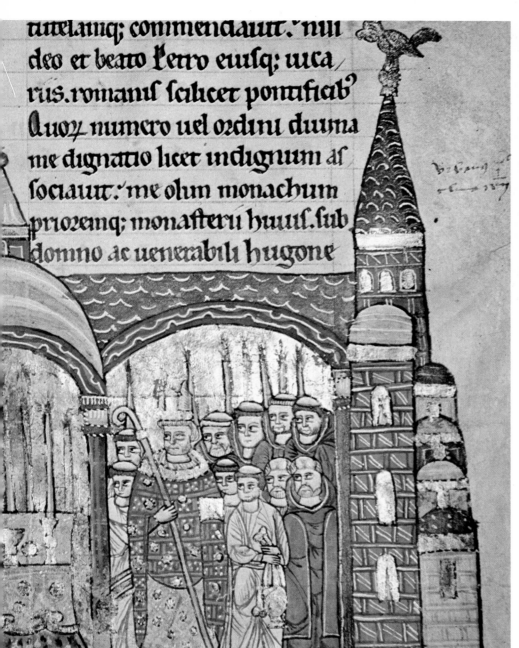

Far left, above, the abbey of Cluny, the birthplace of the most dynamic French monastic movements. Far left, below, the church of Sainte Foy at Conques—one of the most famous pilgrimage churches of medieval France. Near left, the consecration of the main altar at the Cluny abbey in 1095. Above, the abbey of Fontevrault, in the Loire Valley, where early Plantagenet kings of England were buried. Following pages, a scene from the battle between French forces under Philip II and the combined armies of the Holy Roman Empire and England at Bouvines in 1214.

the Île-de-France (the province around Paris), Orléans, and a few other districts—were under the direct rule of the king. The remainder of the realm was divided among feudal lords, who were bound by a theoretical, but not always acknowledged, bond of vassalage to the king and who were unwilling to admit many restrictions to the power they exercised over their lands.

By 950 the disintegration of the royal government and the strength of local particularisms had created a situation in which many local dynasties were able to carve out hereditary principalities for themselves. The appearance of a hereditary nobility, largely unrestrained by royal authority and living off warfare and the labor of the peasants, proved to be one of the most important developments in French history.

Some nobles, such as the duke of Aquitaine and the counts of Flanders and Toulouse, were so independent that at first they did not even recognize the election of Hugh Capet. Indeed the stability of the dynasty was so precarious that until the thirteenth century each king would have his eldest son crowned during his own lifetime to confirm the dynasty's possession of the crown. To make matters worse, the ethnic and linguistic differences that had separated the Western from the Eastern Franks were re-emerging within the West Frankish kingdom. The dialects constituting the *langue d'oc* of the south grew increasingly distinct from the dialects constituting the *langue d'oïl* of the lands north of the Loire. In addition, the inhabitants of the duchy of Brittany and the county of Flanders had their own distinct Celtic and Germanic languages.

The Capetian kings did possess, however, a number

The Albigensian Crusade

In the early thirteenth century, the rich southern province of Languedoc was the center of a Christian heresy known as Catharism, whose followers were often called Albigenses. With papal approval, the barons of northern France launched a holy war against the heretics in 1208. The leader of the crusade, which quickly took on the character of a ruthless war of conquest, was Simon de Montfort. Montfort wrested Béziers and Carcassonne from the Albigenses but was killed during the siege of Toulouse in 1218. By 1226 his heirs had abandoned their father's conquests, which were never returned to their rightful owners and ultimately (in 1271) became part of the French domain. In 1233, Pope Gregory IX created the Inquisition, which effectively stamped out the practices—but not the memory—of the Cathar heresy.

Above right, the fortress of Peyrepertuse, one of the Albigenses' strongholds in Languedoc. Many of these fortresses held out for months against the invaders from northern France, whose crusade has still not been wholly forgiven in Languedoc today. Near right, the cloister of the Church of the Jacobins at Toulouse, the capital of Languedoc. By the thirteenth century, Languedoc was in many ways wealthier and more civilized than northern France. Below, a thirteenth-century miniature showing a soldier cutting out his dead enemy's tongue.

Above, the medieval walled city of Carcassonne. An Albigensian stronghold, Carcassonne was sacked by troops under Simon de Montfort in 1209 and became part of the royal domain in 1246. Right, the Palace of Berbie in Albi. An active center of Catharism, Albi gave the heresy the name by which it is best known—Albigensian.

Above, armed knights of the period in which the Albigensian Crusade was fought.

Below, the seal of Simon de Montfort, a knight from the Île-de-France region who seized the opportunity to gain land and money by leading the crusade against the heretics of Languedoc.

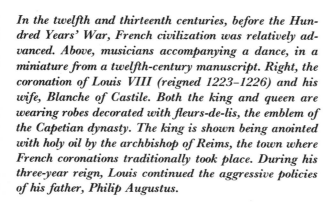

In the twelfth and thirteenth centuries, before the Hundred Years' War, French civilization was relatively advanced. Above, musicians accompanying a dance, in a miniature from a twelfth-century manuscript. Right, the coronation of Louis VIII (reigned 1223–1226) and his wife, Blanche of Castile. Both the king and queen are wearing robes decorated with fleurs-de-lis, the emblem of the Capetian dynasty. The king is shown being anointed with holy oil by the archbishop of Reims, the town where French coronations traditionally took place. During his three-year reign, Louis continued the aggressive policies of his father, Philip Augustus.

of assets. The land they held was the heart of France and included both Paris and Orléans, the keys to the Seine and Loire rivers. As Norman raiders had already discovered, the Capetians' capital at Paris—located on an island in the Seine—was difficult to take, and it had already grown to be one of the largest towns in France. Furthermore, the Capetians were kings, and the title alone was significant in an age steeped in Roman and Carolingian traditions: The monarch inherited the legal powers, and much of the glamour, of the Roman emperors.

The Capetians, members of an indigenous dynasty, wisely restricted themselves to the governance of France alone, and it was this limited aim that made their fortunes and those of the country as a whole. Moreover, they were lucky enough to avoid clashes with the Church while they were consolidating their power—unlike the emperors of Germany, who became embroiled in a bitter controversy with the popes over the right to invest bishops. All too involved with the German emperors, the pope had no wish to enter

into an uncertain struggle with the kings of France. One additional factor favored the Capetians. Unlike many of the lords in the provinces, they had an uninterrupted sequence of male heirs, which enabled the dynasty to prosper for over three centuries without any rancorous disputes over the succession to the throne.

Above all, the Capetian kings had the prestige of being anointed with holy oil and of being the only kings in Christendom believed able to cure "the king's evil," or scrofula. (Even as late as 1775, French peasants waited in thousands to receive Louis XVI's healing touch.) The French monarch, who was called "the most Christian king," was thus a semidivine figure endowed with supernatural attributes, enjoying unrivaled status at a time when Christianity amounted to little more than a jumble of superstitions and heretical beliefs.

From the moment they seized power in 987, the Capetians attempted to strengthen royal authority. On the whole, Hugh Capet's immediate successors

Above, a ball in a garden, as depicted in a medieval manuscript. The women's elaborate headdresses are typical of those worn in the late fourteenth century. Below left, the cathedral of Laon, constructed between 1160 and 1225.

Below, the arrival and distribution of merchandise in a medieval city. Between the twelfth and fourteenth centuries, European commerce grew rapidly and gave birth to an active merchant class, of which the kings were the natural protectors.

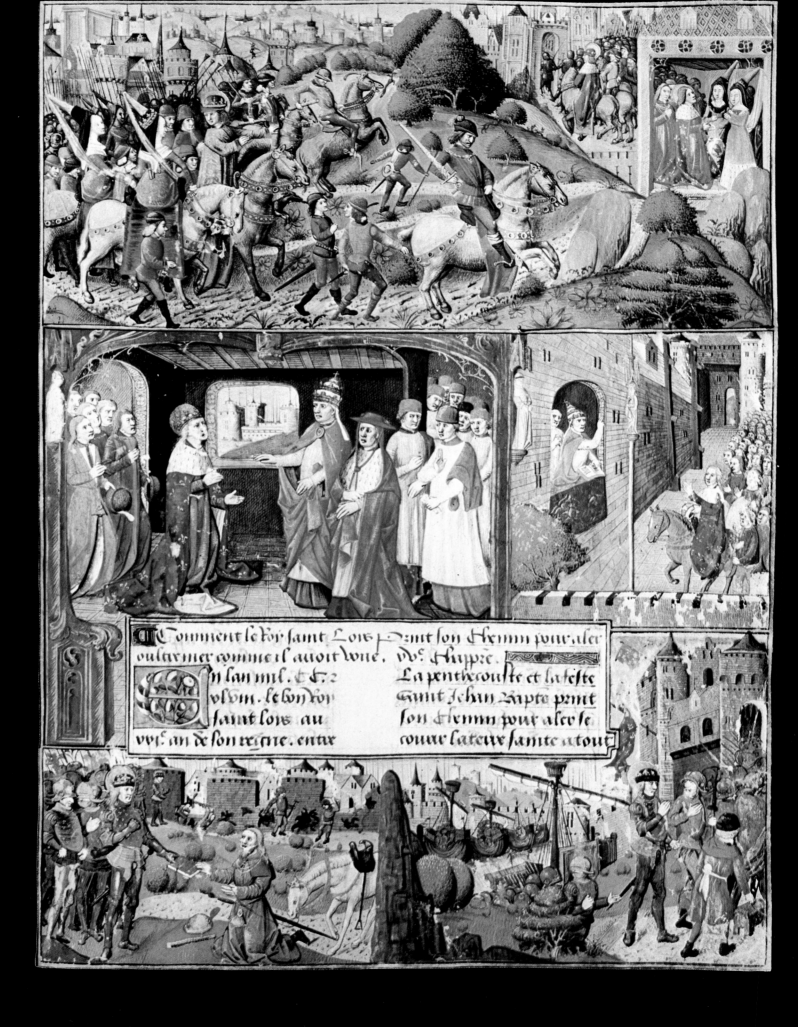

Comment le roy saint Lois prunt son chemin pour aler
oultarmer comme il avoit voue. vie. chapitre.

En l'an mil. ce ce 2   La penthecouste et la feste
vlviii. le bon roy   saint Jehan bapte prunt
saint Lois au   son chemin pour aler se
vie. an de son regne. entra   couuer la terre sainte a tout

accomplished little, but they spared no effort to maintain their inheritance and unwaveringly sought to augment their direct power by wresting fiefs from "rebel" lords and distributing them among younger branches of the family. Sometimes their policies worked well, as when Hugh's second son, Robert the Pious, conquered the important duchy of Burgundy and gave it to his son in 1016. Sometimes they went badly, as when Hugh's grandson Henry I failed in his attempt to defeat William, duke of Normandy; in 1066, William became king of England as William I, thus gaining as much prestige—and considerably more power—than his overlord.

The Capetians continued to pursue their policy of consolidating royal power with vigor and determination in spite of the dislocations produced after 1099 by the Crusades. To this series of expeditions, undertaken in the name of faith and in the hope of obtaining booty, France gave the flower of its nobility, its resources, and its genius. Indeed, in some chronicles the Crusades were characterized as *gesta Dei per Francos:* "divine enterprises achieved by means of the Franks." A French-speaking Christian kingdom, with its capital at Jerusalem, was founded in the late eleventh century on the eastern shore of the Mediterranean, and other French-speaking Crusader states arose in Syria, Greece, and the city of Constantinople. King Louis VI, studiously avoiding service as a Crusader, instead set about organizing a rudimentary tax system at home and enforcing the administration of justice through the Curia Regis, or King's Court. He was much more sensible than his son Louis VII, who spent a good deal of time, effort, and money on a Crusade that did virtually nothing to increase the power or prestige of the Crown.

Louis VII also considerably weakened his position as king by quarreling with his wife, Eleanor of Aquitaine. Heiress of a duchy that comprised almost half the south of France, Eleanor appeared to be an ideal match for Louis. But Eleanor and the pious king proved incompatible. Eleanor failed to produce a male heir, and Louis had the marriage annulled on the pretext that a distant relationship existed between the spouses. A few months later, Eleanor married Louis VII's chief rival, Henry of Anjou, a great-grandson of William I of England. In 1154, Henry became king of England and came into possession of the entire western half of France, including Normandy, Anjou, and much of the Massif Central region. This potentially divisive state of affairs led to a conflict between the two Crowns and gave the initial advantage to the English.

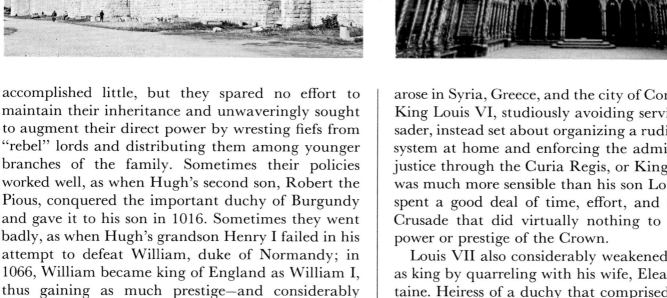

In the course of two centuries the monarchy of the first Capetians had steadily consolidated its authority. Its strength was not yet great, but a central administration was coming into being; the king of France was not yet a powerful monarch, but France was already an influential nation, whose language and culture had been brought to England, Sicily, and the Levant. The period from 1150 to 1400 was a time of French cultural hegemony in Europe. The University of Paris became one of the academic centers of Europe, attracting foreign as well as French students, and Gothic architecture spread from the Île-de-France throughout Europe and to the Crusader states in the Middle East. Nonetheless, the king of France ran the risk of being outshone by his richer cousin, the king of England.

The man who had to confront this peril was the son of Louis VII, Philip II, a king who after his death in 1223 was given the title of Philip Augustus. Philip's greatest accomplishment is commemorated in his epitaph: *ampliavit fines regni* ("he enlarged the boundaries of the kingdom"). He reconquered the Vermandois district in the north by diplomacy and retook the Anjou, Maine, and Normandy regions by force of arms. Philip's victory at Bouvines in northeastern France in 1214 humiliated the combined forces of England and the Holy Roman Empire.

Philip Augustus was not only a successful war leader. During his reign the administration of the country was improved through the use of "bailiffs" and "seneschals," who represented the authority of the king in the provinces. (The most prestigious of-

Immediately below, Philip III (reigned 1270–1285) teaching the divine commandment to "love in the name of the Lord." This miniature reflects the extent to which the king of France was a religious as well as a political figure. The religious aura surrounding the kings of France was naturally enhanced by the canonization of Louis IX in 1297.

Above, the papal palace in Avignon. Between 1309 and 1377, Avignon was the seat of the most international institution of the Middle Ages—the papacy.

Left, Philip IV (reigned 1285–1314) seated on his throne. Philip, a capable and despotic king, consolidated the hold of the Capetian kings over France and established his authority in ecclesiastical matters over the papacy. In 1309, under Philip IV, the papacy was transferred from Rome to Avignon.

Above, a medieval building in Meaux, a town northeast of Paris. Meaux is in a fertile wheat-growing province that figured prominently in the Jacquerie, or peasant revolt of 1358. The insurrection was a reaction against the excessive burdens placed on the peasantry during the Hundred Years' War. Right, the entrance of Charles V (reigned 1364–1380) into Paris in 1364. Under Charles' leadership, France reconquered almost all French territory previously held by the English.

Left, John II (reigned 1350–1364) founding the Order of the Star in 1352. John, the second Valois king of France, was repeatedly defeated by the English during the Hundred Years' War.

fices were left unfilled so that their holders could not threaten the king.) The position of the monarch was reinforced to such an extent that by the thirteenth century monarchs no longer felt it necessary to crown the heir to the throne while the reigning king was still alive. Philip Augustus, the king of the Franks, assumed for himself and his descendants the title of king of France—an appellation his successors were to bear proudly for the next six hundred years.

After the three-year reign of Louis VIII, the crown passed in 1226 to the grandson of Philip Augustus, Louis IX. Louis IX inherited one of the principal kingdoms in Christendom, one that was beginning to conduct a considerable amount of commerce with other countries and to develop a sizable urban population. A flourishing economy even enabled the mint to produce a stable coinage for the first time.

Under Louis IX the Capetians reached new heights of power and prestige. His younger brother won lands and crowns in Italy and the Middle East, and the king of England was forced to cede more of his dominions to France. Two Crusades led by Louis himself (the second of which cost him his life in 1270) revived the tradition of French monarchs as champions of militant Christendom and led to the king's canonization. During his reign, this pious ruler issued several edicts against the immorality of his worldly capital and built the Sainte-Chapelle in Paris to shelter holy relics brought back from the Crusades.

Louis' son, Philip III, was a pious but weak sovereign. Philip's successor, Philip IV, who reigned from 1285 to 1314, was the last of the great Capetian kings. Philip attacked the power of the Church (whose tithes he pocketed) and suppressed the order known as the

Above, the battle of Sluis (1340), in which the French fleet was almost completely decimated by the English. Below, the murder of a noble by peasants in revolt.

Knights Templars in order to seize its fabulous treasures and lucrative estates. To facilitate the raising of taxes he founded the States-General, a legislative institution that was soon to exhibit a desire for power of its own. Under Philip the great law court, the Parlement of Paris, split off from the Curia Regis and began to assert its autonomy.

The kingdom of France was still a very fragile state during this period. And the house founded by Hugh Capet was about to experience its first disputed succession, endangering all that had been built up during centuries of statecraft and warfare.

Philip IV died in 1314. With the death of his son Louis X and infant grandson two years later, the crown of France was without direct male heirs. It might have been given to the last king's sister, but a law dating from the legendary times of the Franks excluded women from the succession. Instead the crown passed to the younger brother of Louis X, then to another brother, and finally to Philip VI, a prince of a younger branch of the family. This marked the beginning of a new reigning house, the Valois.

Edward III of England, who also claimed the throne of France, was not about to miss this glorious opportunity for making trouble in France. Edward's adoption of the title of king of France and the addition of the Capetians' fleur-de-lis to his coat of arms— both of which were retained by the kings of England until 1802—demonstrated his desire to acquire the incomparable prestige and extensive territory of his French cousin. In 1339, English troops disembarked on the Continent. The wars that followed, known as the Hundred Years' War, lasted until 1453.

Joan of Arc

Above, Joan of Arc driving the bawds away from the French army.

Below, the house in the village of Domrémy where Joan was born in 1412. Below left, a detail of a page from a fifteenth-century manuscript showing the only known picture of Joan done during her lifetime.

In 1429 the position of France in the Hundred Years' War was desperate. Aided by their Burgundian allies, the English had gained control of the province of Gascony and most of France north of the Loire. In February of that year, however, a shepherd girl named Joan of Arc from the village of Domrémy, claiming to have heard "heavenly voices," managed to meet with the dauphin at the town of Chinon. Joan inspired him with new courage and—in what seemed a miracle to some of her contemporaries—herself raised the seven-month English siege of Orléans in May 1429. A year later she escorted the dauphin to Reims, where he was crowned king of France in the traditional rite. The English were never able to retake the offensive, even after Joan was captured by the Burgundians and burned alive as a witch—with the blessing of the Church—at Rouen in 1431.

Joan of Arc, who in 1920 was proclaimed a saint, is still one of the most powerful symbols of French nationalism. In 1940, General Charles De Gaulle adopted her Cross of Lorraine as the emblem of the forces of Free France.

Above, the port of Brest under siege by the constable of France, Bertrand Du Guesclin, who reorganized the French army under Charles V and helped drive out the English in the 1360s and 1370s. Right, the arrival of Joan of Arc at Chinon, the dauphin's favorite residence in the Loire Valley.

Below, the tower in which Joan was imprisoned before her execution on May 30, 1431. Below right, a miniature depicting Joan of Arc at the stake. Captured by the Burgundians and handed over to the English, Joan was condemned by an ecclesiastical tribunal to be burned at the stake.

Left, Burgundians slaughtering Armagnacs in Paris in 1418. Struggles between the Burgundian and Armagnac factions—supporters of two branches of the royal house of France—tragically weakened the country in the early fifteenth century, during the Hundred Years' War.

Below, the portico of the cathedral of Saint-Étienne at Bourges, an ancient city in central France. Bourges was one of the chief strongholds of Charles VII at the beginning of his reign.

The wars against the English devastated France, which only a few years before had been the richest and most powerful country in Europe. Nearly all the fighting was done on French soil, as is evident from the names of the great English victories: Crécy (1346), Poitiers (1356), and Agincourt (1415). France's armies were defeated and its nobility divided into warring factions, often more ready to help the enemy than their own kings.

No longer could the envious Germans say "as rich as God in France." The countryside was ravaged by bands of pillaging troops eager for plunder. The suffering peasantry, oppressed by serfdom, forced labor, mercenary bands, and feudal lords, broke out in a savage rebellion known as the Jacquerie. The population decreased drastically, not only because of the warfare but also because of the devastating plagues that swept through all of Europe during the fourteenth century.

In 1356, John II of France was taken as a prisoner to England. John was succeeded in 1364 by Charles V, his son, who led France in a dramatic recovery from the Hundred Years' War. Charles, known to history as "the Wise," restored internal peace to France, helped re-establish monarchical dignity, and encouraged the development of art and literature. But in 1414, during the reign of Charles VI, Charles V's deranged son, the English invaded France again. Within six years they had gained control of Paris and the king. Charles VI's son, denounced by his own mother as a bastard, was forced to take refuge in the Loire Valley where, after his father's death in 1422,

Right, a page from a fifteenth-century manuscript showing Charles VI being presented with a book. The reign of Charles VI (1380-1422), the eldest son of Charles V, was a period of decline for the monarchy. The king, who was subject to increasingly serious attacks of madness, proved incapable of keeping a firm hold on the government of the country. The duke of Burgundy, Charles' cousin, engaged in a fierce struggle for power with Charles' younger brother and the Armagnac faction. Both sides were all too ready to ally themselves with the English during the Hundred Years' War.

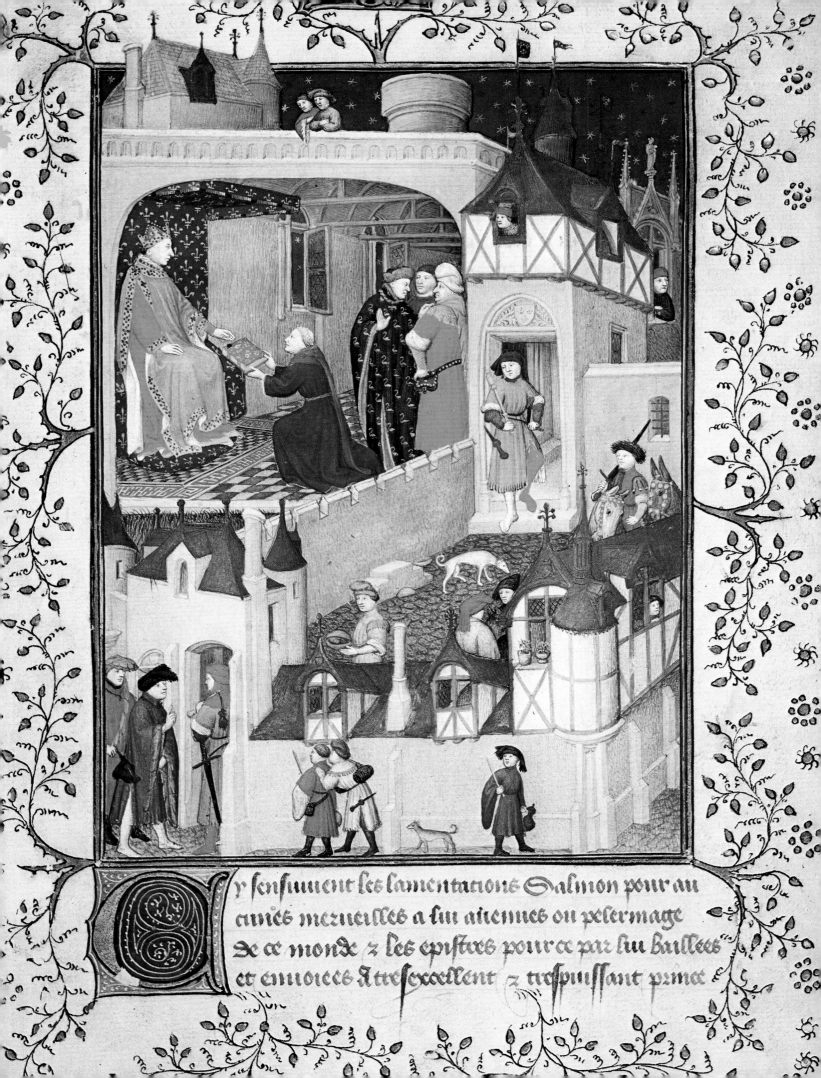

y senfuinent les lamentations Salmon pour au
cunes mezueilles a lin auennes en pelermage
de ce monde z les epistres pour ce par lui baillees
et ennoiees a tresexcellent z trespuissant prince

Top, a portrait of Charles VII (reigned 1422–1461). Above, a coin of Charles VII, showing the fleurs-de-lis emblem of the kings of France. Right, the battle of Agincourt (1415), which demonstrated the effectiveness of archers against heavily armed warriors.

he assumed the title of king. By 1429 it seemed that if the English could take the city of Orléans, even the few remaining provinces left to the uncrowned Charles VII would fall to their armies.

The English siege of Orléans, however, was raised by Joan of Arc, a girl from the Lorraine region, whose fervor and vision gave strength to the French cause. Soon Joan helped lead Charles to Reims for his coronation. Charles, aided by skilled advisers and able generals, was able to take Paris by 1436 and all the English possessions in France except Calais by 1453.

Charles did not just recover territory, though. During his reign the Crown won the right to raise direct taxes—especially the taille, which fell largely on the peasants—without the consent of the States-General and first established a permanent standing army. War thus proved to be the surest means of giving French monarchs the authority necessary to expand royal power in the kingdom. Monarchical authority increased still more under Charles' astute son Louis XI, who in 1477 annexed Burgundy, a duchy controlled by a branch of the Valois hostile to France. He also inherited Provence four years later.

While France and England were engaged in fighting the Hundred Years' War, important changes were

Left, Charles VIII (reigned 1483–1498). The kingdom Charles inherited from his father, Louis XI (reigned 1461–1483), was extremely rich and remarkably obedient. Charles continued his ancestors' tradition of interfering in Italian affairs, hoping to conquer the kingdom of Naples at the very least.

Below, the castle of Foix in the Pyrenees. Foix was the center of a small lordship that functioned as a semi-independent unit in the fifteenth century.

taking place in Europe. In Italy the Renaissance was beginning its civilizing task. Further east, the Turks had delivered the last blow to the thousand-year-old Eastern Roman Empire and had launched their campaign into the Balkans. And by 1500 the French faced a peril even graver than England: the Hapsburg Empire. As the result of a series of fortunate marriages the Hapsburgs were about to add the Netherlands, the Franche-Comté (in the east-central part of present-day France), and Spain to their hereditary lands in Austria and the Tyrolean region. Confronted on all sides by Hapsburg troops, officials, and lands, the French took decisive action.

In 1494, Charles VIII, the son of Louis XI, invaded Italy to claim the crown of Naples, which had at one time belonged to his ancestors of the House of Anjou. He entered Naples in triumph, with the insignia of a Roman emperor carried before him. French armies fared poorly in subsequent years, however, until the youthful, aggressive, and self-confident Francis I ascended the throne in 1515. In his fight against Charles V, the Hapsburg Holy Roman emperor, Francis I lavished everything: his army, his subjects' taxes, and his own person. His victory at Marignano in northern Italy in 1515 brought Lombardy under French control for a decade. Defeated ten years later

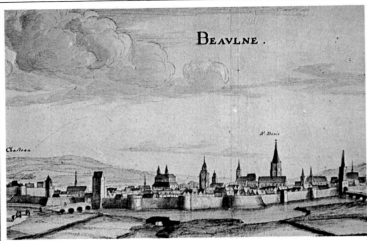

BEAVLNE.

The duchy of Burgundy

In the fifteenth century, a heterogeneous but powerful state ruled by a collateral branch of the House of Valois arose on the borders between France and the Holy Roman Empire. By 1450 it included the richest provinces of the Low Countries—Flanders and Brabant—and many other regions acquired through annexation, purchase, or inheritance. The dukes of Burgundy, nominally vassals of the king of France and the Holy Roman emperor but in reality completely independent of both, created a dynamic state and directly threatened the kings of France. Their fragmented state collapsed, however, when the fourth duke of Burgundy, known because of his reckless aggression as Charles the Bold, fell in the battle of Nancy (1477).

The dominions of the dukes of Burgundy were subsequently divided between the Hapsburgs and France. The history of Burgundy for the next two hundred years was fated to be a stormy one. The duchy was ravaged during the Catholic-Protestant wars of the sixteenth century, again during the Thirty Years' War (1618–1648), and still again during the aristocratic revolt against Cardinal Mazarin and the French court in the mid-seventeenth century. Peace and order were restored only in the final quarter of the seventeenth century.

Left, a detail from a picture of the duke of Burgundy hunting. Because the duke of Burgundy was neither a king nor an emperor, he needed to bolster his prestige by the pomp and splendor of his court.

Above, the Parlement of Burgundy meeting in the presence of Charles the Bold. Below, a manuscript being presented to Philip the Good, father of Charles the Bold.

at Pavia (south of Milan) in a memorable battle that—as he wrote to his mother—cost him everything except his honor and his life, Francis was taken prisoner; he was freed only after being exchanged for his sons.

Soon after his release, Francis took up arms again and made fresh alliances against his hated rival—concluding an agreement with the Turks in 1536 so as to threaten the Hapsburgs from the rear. A king more interested in military glory than in the welfare of his subjects, Francis was prepared to be called "the most Christian Turk in Paris" to ensure French predominance in Europe. It was fortunate that he did not live to see the Peace of Cateau-Cambrésis, negotiated in 1559, which confirmed France's failure to make any lasting war conquests except for Calais and three towns in Alsace.

Under Francis I, commerce expanded and the city of Lyon on the Rhône River became a major banking and trading center. Many rich nonnobles acquired nobles' estates and were subsequently absorbed into the nobility. In addition, Francis instituted a change in policy that allowed nonnobles to easily change their status. He started selling offices in the royal administration—offices that conferred nobility on their holders.

Right, the hedgehog, the personal symbol of Louis XII (reigned 1498–1515). The hedgehog is a frequent decorative motif on the walls of the Louis XII wing of the chateau at Blois in the Loire Valley. Below, the great outside staircase of the chateau at Blois.

Francis displayed a great love for the arts, especially those that enhanced his own prestige. He brought Leonardo da Vinci and many other Italian artists to France and enlarged and embellished his favorite chateau of Fontainebleau. At this royal residence a school of artists developed that directly reflected the influence of the Italian Renaissance. In fact, Francis' court was the most magnificent of the day, a uniquely civilizing center of power and pleasure, where at least a few women were treated as the social and intellectual equals of men and where the manners of the nobility in time became increasingly refined.

At his death in 1547, Francis was one of the most celebrated monarchs in Europe. His heirs were not of his caliber, but then they did not have the benefit of the remarkably united and obedient kingdom Francis had inherited from his predecessors. Among the forces that had most aided Francis in his fight against Charles V had been the Protestant Reformation, a movement that started in Germany in the first quarter of the sixteenth century. During Francis' reign, German Protestant princes had been delighted to ally themselves with the king of France against the Catholic Hapsburgs. But after 1550 the French Protestants—known as Huguenots—became even more nu-

Above, Louis XII. Louis' wise internal policies earned him the title "father of the people."

Right, Louis XII leading his knights in an attack on Genoa. Louis, who hoped to control the papacy and conquer Naples, succeeded only in wasting French men and money. Exhausted by the attentions of his young English wife (a sister of Henry VIII), he died in 1515.

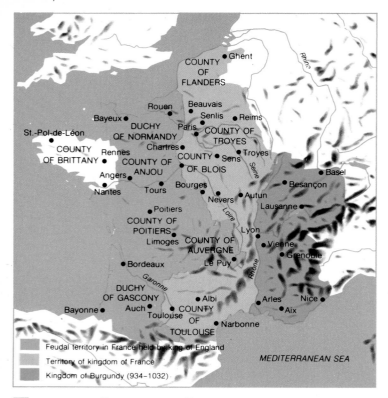

France during the tenth and eleventh centuries

In the tenth and eleventh centuries, most of the area now known as France was controlled by three kingdoms. England governed the western section, and the independent kingdom of Burgundy held sway in the east. The central region—the kingdom of France—was ruled by the Carolingian dynasty until 987, when the crown passed to Hugh Capet, the first king of the Capetian line. Monarchs in a feudal realm, the Capetian kings attempted to counter the influence of powerful barons by extending the royal domain—the land owned directly by the sovereign or his knights. This spread royal authority thin throughout the realm, however, and in effect abetted the fractious barons. Hugh's great-grandson Philip I (reigned 1060–1108) met with some success in consolidating royal authority but was persistently defied by his vassals.

France at the death of Philip Augustus, 1223

Philip II, known as Philip Augustus (reigned 1180–1223), extended the boundaries of the French kingdom, reclaiming Normandy and Anjou, among other provinces, from the English. Although annexed to France, the captured regions were allowed to retain their customs and administrative institutions. The wisdom of this leniency was borne out in the century following Philip's death, as the kings of France continued his policies.

France in 1659

Louis XIV (reigned 1643–1715) is remembered as an absolute monarch, yet the control he exercised over his realm was far from uncontested or solitary. The kingdom was plagued with internal divisions, with the power of the provinces and the local nobility still challenging monarchical authority. In foreign policy, Louis was capably aided by Cardinal Jules Mazarin until the cardinal's death in 1661. It was Mazarin who negotiated the Treaty of the Pyrenees in 1659, which awarded France territory in the north and south. A pact concluded in 1648 had already ceded to France the bishoprics of Metz, Toul, and Verdun, as well as a number of small towns in Alsace.

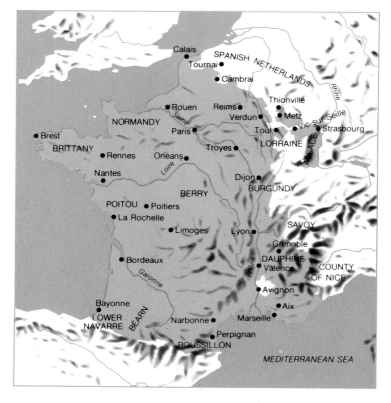

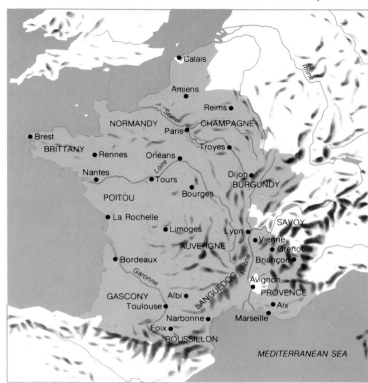

France during the Hundred Years' War

The protracted conflict between the French and English called the Hundred Years' War (1337–1453) was fought almost entirely on French soil. Ravaged by English raids and the plague, France met with little success in the opening rounds of the war and was decisively defeated at Agincourt in 1415. By war's end, however, Charles VII had succeeded in expelling the English from most of France. The English were completely ousted from France in 1558.

France of Louis XI, 1461-1483

Louis XI largely succeeded in his tireless efforts to increase monarchical authority. An ambitious and unscrupulous ruler, Louis effectively countered the threat of a princely constitution and thus destroyed any hope for provincial independence against royal centralization. To help consolidate his position, Louis fomented strife between Normandy and Brittany, recovering Normandy from his brother and isolating Brittany. He long focused his diplomacy on Burgundy and encouraged a coalition of the Swiss cantons and Austria to invade the province. When Charles the Bold, duke of Burgundy, was killed in battle in 1477, Louis seized as much of the Burgundian inheritance as possible. France's boundaries were further extended when Provence and several other territories were escheated to the Crown in 1480.

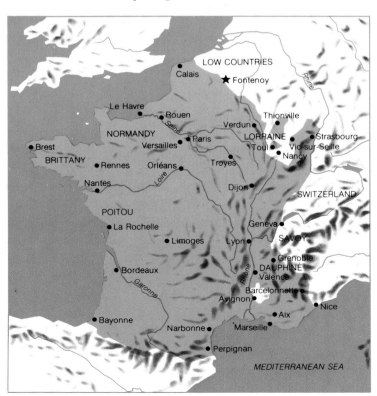

France in 1765

The relationship between society and state that existed at the time of Louis XV's accession in 1715 was destroyed because the monarchy proved unwilling to accept the rapid economic, intellectual, and social changes of eighteenth-century France. In foreign relations, the monarchy viewed any change in the existing order as contrary to its vested interests. As part of Louis XV's efforts to maintain the balance of power in Europe, France allied itself with Prussia in the War of the Austrian Succession (1740–1748); in a famous battle fought in 1745, the French defeated a combined force at Fontenoy. The monarchy's insistence on preserving the status quo culminated in the Revolution.

Left, Francis I (reigned 1515–1547), cousin and son-in-law of Louis XII. Right, Francis' second wife, Eleanor of Austria, sister of Charles V. Below right, Claude of Lorraine, the first duke of Guise and one of Francis' most trusted generals. Facing page, the chateau of Fontainebleau, the favorite residence of Francis I: the courtyard façade (above), the Francis I gallery (below left), and the ballroom (below right).

merous, creating a divisive force within France. Soon entire regions, especially in the south, were Huguenot-dominated, and one branch of the royal family itself, the Bourbons, was converted to the "heresy."

The rift between Catholics and Protestants, each of which soon became a political faction determined to dominate or defy the king, grew increasingly tragic and violent. The question was not only one of rival magnates out for their own ends, like the Armagnacs and the Burgundians, who two centuries earlier had almost brought about the ruin of the country in the face of the English invasion. Now thousands of ordinary Protestants and Catholics were prepared to fight for the cause of their religion.

In 1559, Henry II, the son of Francis I, died in a tournament and left the realm to his young and sickly son Francis II, who was in turn succeeded by his brother Charles IX in 1560. A dominant figure in politics during this period was the queen mother, Catherine de Médicis, an ambitious and intelligent Florentine who throughout her sons' reigns used the splendor of her court—and, occasionally, the charms of her maids of honor—to bolster the authority of the Crown. At first she hoped to lure the Huguenots back to the Catholic Church by a program of reform, but both sides proved averse to conciliation. In 1572 the growing influence that the Huguenot admiral Gaspard de Coligny gained over the king provoked a violent Catholic reaction.

On August 22, Coligny was wounded in the arm by a hired gunman. Two days later the leader of the Catholic faction, the popular Henry of Guise, sent one of his followers to Coligny's house to finish the admiral off. Coligny's mutilated body was flung from

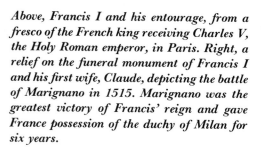

Above, Francis I and his entourage, from a fresco of the French king receiving Charles V, the Holy Roman emperor, in Paris. Right, a relief on the funeral monument of Francis I and his first wife, Claude, depicting the battle of Marignano in 1515. Marignano was the greatest victory of Francis' reign and gave France possession of the duchy of Milan for six years.

the window—the prearranged signal for a massacre. Thousands of presumed heretics were shot, lynched, or dragged naked through the streets and beaten to death. Protestant courtiers were cut down in the royal antechambers. In six hours at least two thousand people were butchered in Paris alone. But this bloody episode, known as the Massacre of St. Bartholomew's Day, not only failed to eradicate the "heresy" but fueled further outbreaks of civil war.

In 1574, Charles IX followed his Huguenot subjects to the grave, and his younger brother, who had been king of Poland for two years, ascended the throne as Henry III. It was plain that the new king

would have to make concessions to the Huguenot faction, which controlled numerous fortresses and whole provinces in the south. It was just as evident that such a policy would not appeal to the Catholics, who were led by Henry of Guise, the magnetic and forceful head of a family that was seeking to dominate—and perhaps replace—the unpopular king. Guise's ambitions gained support because the king, having no direct heirs, was to be succeeded by Henry of Bourbon, king of Navarre—and leader of the Huguenots. (Henry of Bourbon had escaped the Massacre of St. Bartholomew's Day only by abjuring his faith under duress; once he returned to his kingdom

Left, the 1519 meeting between Henry VIII of England and Francis I of France on the "Field of the Cloth of Gold" outside Calais—at the time an English possession. The encounter between the two kings proved to have little political significance, since the planned alliance against Charles V, the Holy Roman emperor, did not materialize. In fact, Henry VIII not long afterward signed an agreement with Charles V in his efforts to press English claims to the throne of France.

Below, a view of the city of Calais in 1538. Calais, the last remaining English possession on the Continent, was lost to France in 1558. Following pages, the entry of Henry II into Rouen in 1550.

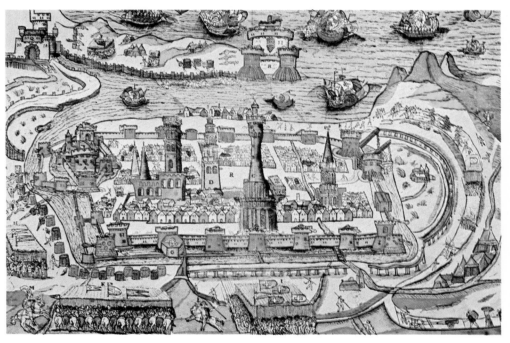

in the Pyrenees he took up his former religion again.) Henry of Guise's position was further strengthened by his leadership of the Holy League, a Catholic organization with fervent support among the urban masses, and by a secret alliance with Spain.

On December 23, 1588, Henry of Guise was assassinated by some of the king's guards while waiting for a council meeting in the king's bedroom. When Henry III came to look at the corpse of his chief adversary, he exclaimed: *"Mon Dieu!* How large he is! He seems even larger dead than alive." The king proved to be correct, since most of France, including Paris, soon revolted against the perfidious monarch who had murdered their hero. Less than a year later, Henry III fell to the dagger of a fanatical monk, Jacques Clément.

Like the Capetians before them, the Valois line had ended in three brothers who were all kings. The question now arose: Could Henry of Bourbon, the Huguenot king of Navarre, succeed to the sacred crown of Clovis, Charlemagne, and Saint Louis? Most Frenchmen thought not, and the Holy League, still led by members of the Guise family and by this point supported by Spanish troops actually in France, remained in control of much of the kingdom. Religious

Diane de Poitiers, mistress

Diane de Poitiers, who became the mistress of Henry II while he was still the dauphin, exercised great influence over the king throughout his reign. She rarely left the king's side and advertised her status at the lavish entertainments she gave for the court and foreign ambassadors. In politics, Diane de Poitiers tended to support the Montmorency family—one of the oldest families in France and traditionally loyal to the Crown—against the increasingly prestigious House of Guise.

Henry's queen, Catherine de Médicis, endured the presence of Diane de Poitiers while her husband was alive. But after the king's death in 1559, she took her revenge by seizing for herself Diane de Poitiers' favorite chateau, Chenonceaux. Thereafter, Diane de Poitiers was forced to live in complete retirement.

Above, a portrait of Henry II (reigned 1547–1559). Gloomy and introspective, Henry spent four years in a Spanish prison as a hostage for his father's observance of a treaty with Charles V, the Hapsburg who reigned as Holy Roman emperor from 1519 to 1556. As king, Henry continued his father's anti-Hapsburg policy. He left to his heirs a kingdom dangerously divided into factions supporting the great families of Guise, Bourbon, and Montmorency.

Above, Catherine de Médicis. After the death of her husband, Henry II, in 1559, she acted as regent for her sons Charles IX and Henry III. Above right, a parade in honor of Henry II at Rouen. All the parades and pageantry of the later Valois could not, however, hide their increasing powerlessness. Right, sixteenth-century houses in Rouen.

faith and party spirit proved stronger than dynastic loyalty and patriotism.

In the end, Henry IV chose the only possible solution. In 1593—perhaps making the famous remark "Paris is worth a mass"—he converted to Catholicism, and the next year he cheerfully entered his capital.

The kingdom Henry inherited had almost as many problems as subjects. Towns, districts, and provinces throughout France, often encouraged by local nobles, had become accustomed to behaving as their own masters. The Protestants in particular had an army of twenty-five thousand men that could be mustered at a moment's notice, as well as their own fortresses and tax system; in effect, they constituted a state within a state.

Once again, as after the Hundred Years' War, royal authority had to be reasserted in a chaotic and embittered kingdom. But Henry IV was a king equal to the task. A tough, brave, down-to-earth soldier, he possessed a self-confidence and joie de vivre that were up to the standards of Francis I. Above all, in a soci-

ety that placed a high value on military success, Henry was a monarch who combined the appeal of hereditary right with the glory of victory on the battlefield. In the 1590s the last rebellious provinces and nobles rallied to the side of the king. In 1598, Henry promulgated the Edict of Nantes, a law that gave the Huguenots considerable legal and political rights and ended the terrible religious wars. But even after the religious strife had ceased, the nobles—particularly the members of the houses of Guise and Montmorency and certain of the king's cousins, such as the princes de Condé and de Conti—still had to be flattered, bribed, and lured to court so that they would not use their provincial power bases and foreign contacts to stir up trouble for the king.

After 1598, France began to recover from the decades of turmoil. In a somewhat haphazard way internal peace was restored, agriculture and trade encouraged, revenues increased, and the debt diminished. The country was so rich in human and material resources that, once free of internal strife and

Above, the Massacre of St. Bartholomew's Day, the bloodiest episode of the wars fought between Catholics and Protestants (Huguenots) in sixteenth-century France. The Crown generally tolerated the Protestants. But in 1572, alarmed at the growing influence of Admiral Gaspard de Coligny, a Protestant leader, Catherine de Médicis obtained the permission of Charles IX for this massacre.

Right, Charles IX (reigned 1560–1574). Charles' reign saw a worsening of the conflict between Catholics and Protestants in France and a decline in the power and authority of the Crown. He had no sons from his marriage with a Hapsburg, Elizabeth of Austria.

exhausting wars, it revived almost of its own accord. The duke of Sully, Henry IV's chief minister, especially encouraged the revival of agriculture, calling plowing and grazing "the two breasts of France."

Responding to the ever-present threat of encirclement by the Hapsburgs, Henry decided in 1610 to attack the Hapsburgs in the Low Countries with the aid of German Protestants. He never, though, had the opportunity to put his plans into practice. On May 14, 1610, Henry—who had always said that the same crowds cheering him so readily would be just as eager to tear him to pieces—was assassinated by François Ravaillac, a Catholic fanatic.

Henry IV was succeeded by his son Louis XIII, who was only nine years old; Louis' mother, Marie de Médicis, acted as regent. The melancholic and introspective Louis was markedly different from his exuberant and self-assured father. The earlier part of Louis' reign was marred by a series of bloody civil wars, usually led by members of his own family: his cousin the prince de Condé, his brother Gaston d'Orléans (whose name, even at the French court, was a byword for treachery), or his own mother. Understandably wary of his own family, Louis ignored his mother's threats and pleas and in 1632 confirmed the appointment of Cardinal Richelieu as his chief minister. Although often annoyed or displeased by the domineering Richelieu, Louis retained confidence in him to the end.

Richelieu was dedicated to increasing the power of the Crown. Under his guidance, Louis XIII turned away from the policies of peace, retrenchment, and reform advocated by his mother and the Catholic faction and devoted all his energies to defeating his enemies at home and abroad. Rebellious—or simply discontented—nobles were fought or intimidated whenever possible. In the provinces, professional officials responsible to the king, among them the detested administrators known as intendants, were appointed to complement the governors drawn from the higher nobility. Although their religious rights were maintained, the Huguenots were forced to surrender their strongholds and the political rights that enabled them to act as a state within a state. (The cardinal himself did not hesitate to mount his charger and lead the assault on the mightiest Huguenot stronghold, La Rochelle.) A true central bureaucracy was in the process of formation, and Louis XIII and Richelieu proved to be undoubtedly the most effective rulers France had yet known.

But like most of those who had governed France since the time of Francis I, Richelieu was concerned

Left, a procession of the Holy League through the streets of Paris, organized to demand the defeat of the Huguenots. The Holy League reached the height of its power between 1585 and 1594. Headed by the Guise family and aided by Spain, it controlled much of France and dominated Paris. Above, Francis II (reigned 1559–1560), the first husband of Mary Queen of Scots. During Francis' reign the duke of Guise, the queen's uncle, dominated the government.

Left, a tournament at the court of Henry III (reigned 1574–1589), the third of Henry II's sons to succeed to the throne of France. The figure on the right is the king's younger brother Francis, duke of Alençon, whose revolts and intrigues seriously weakened the Crown during Henry's reign. The figure on the left is William of Orange, an advocate of French intervention in the Low Countries against the Spanish.

Below, the young Henry III, the last Valois king of France. Forced by French Protestants to grant them a certain measure of freedom and autonomy, he attracted the anger of Catholics and was assassinated by a fanatical Dominican friar.

chiefly with the Hapsburg possessions surrounding France. His strategy aimed at recovering some of the territories that Charlemagne had once ruled beyond France's eastern frontier and at depriving potential rebels of an ever-willing refuge and ally. Although a cardinal of the Roman Catholic Church, Richelieu allied himself with the Lutheran king of Sweden, Gustavus Adolphus, who was the leader of the German Protestant princes' struggle against their Hapsburg emperor. In Switzerland and Italy, French forces intervened to break the hegemony of Spain, attempting to sever contact between the Austrian and Spanish branches of the Hapsburgs. Meanwhile Ri-

chelieu built up a navy capable of challenging the Spanish fleet and the English and Dutch merchant navies.

The cost of Richelieu's ambitions was enormous. Taxation became an intolerable burden for most Frenchmen, and revolts, often encouraged by local officeholders or Parlements, erupted throughout France in the 1630s and 1640s. At times almost the whole of the south of France, always the area of strongest provincial feeling, was in rebellion against the Crown, and in 1636 the Spanish army nearly took Paris. When Louis XIII died in 1643, full of remorse at the suffering and hardship he had caused his peo-

Below, Gabrielle d'Estrées (right) and her sister. Gabrielle d'Estrées was the most important mistress of Henry IV in the 1590s and exerted considerable political influence. Her sister's gesture is probably a reference to the fact that Gabrielle d'Estrées was about to bear the king a child.

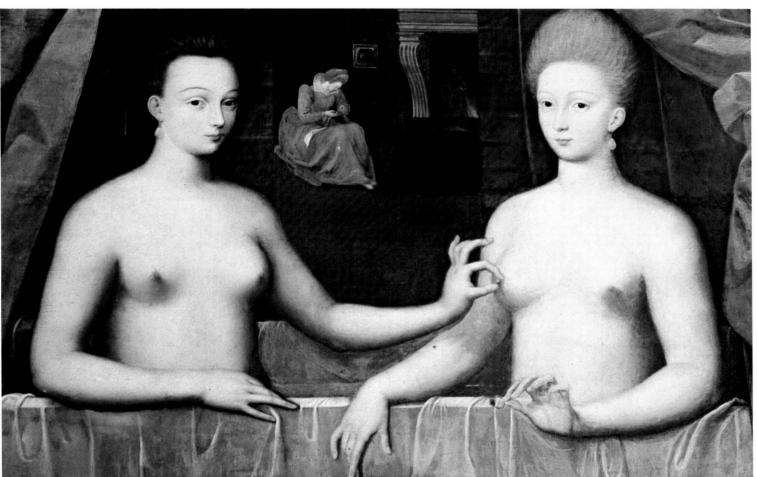

ple, he left behind a dangerous legacy of bitterness and discontent.

When Louis XIV succeeded his father to the throne at the age of five, the young king's mother, Anne of Austria, became the third foreign queen in a hundred years to serve as regent. Her chief minister was Cardinal Jules Mazarin, a flexible and unfailingly ingenious Italian who had started his career as a papal diplomat and nuncio but later entered the more rewarding service of the king of France. A protégé of Richelieu, Mazarin was nonetheless quite different from his great predecessor: Whereas Riche-

lieu sent his enemies to the Bastille, Mazarin tried to bribe them. But if their methods of repression varied, their basic policies were identical. Both worked for the reduction of aristocratic power, the creation of a civil service owing obedience only to the king and his ministers and maintaining effective control in the provinces, and the suppression of local rights and privileges. They also pursued a foreign policy that attempted to erode the power of the Hapsburgs.

However, the resistance of the aristocracy and Parlements, determined to retain and if possible increase their privileges, gave birth to the Fronde: a series of civil wars, provincial revolts, and court in-

Above, the first page of the document that made Henry IV's first wife, Marie de Médicis, regent for Louis XIII after Henry's assassination.

Left, the armor of Henry IV. Above, Rubens' painting of the coronation of Marie de Médicis in 1610. (Henry IV is depicted watching from a balcony.) This ceremony—the last at which a queen of France was crowned—was intended to give added prestige to Marie, who was to act as regent for her husband while he led foreign campaigns. Henry was murdered, however, shortly thereafter, and Marie became regent for her son.

Below, the Palais de Justice in Paris. Originally the king's principal residence, by the sixteenth century these buildings had become the seat of France's main law court. Right, the first page of the Edict of Nantes, promulgated by Henry IV in 1598, which guaranteed full rights to the French Protestants.

trigues lasting from 1648 to 1653. Mazarin was twice forced to flee abroad, and in 1648 the court had to leave Paris in the middle of the night. In a famous incident that took place in 1652, Louis XIV's first cousin, a daughter of Gaston d'Orléans, turned the cannons of the Bastille on the royal army, which was trying to recapture Paris.

Yet Mazarin triumphed in the end. He succeeded in dividing his rivals, liquidating the Fronde, and making an advantageous peace with Spain that gave Louis XIV a dull wife and France the provinces of Roussillon and Artois. When Mazarin died in 1661—heartbroken at having to leave his beautiful palace and vast collections of jewels, sculpture, and paintings—there was no doubt that France was what the Bourbons and their ministers had always wished it to be: the first power in Europe. After a long apprenticeship under Mazarin, it was now up to the king, who was only twenty-two, to exploit that inheritance to the full.

Nearly everyone assumed that Louis would choose someone to assume Mazarin's post, and few, if any, believed it when the king declared that from then on he would be his own prime minister. However, until the very last day of his reign in 1715—the longest reign in European history—Louis XIV was the effective ruler of France as well as the director and lead actor in the magnificent daily ritual of his own kingship. Blessed with an iron constitution and a seemingly indestructible physique, he enjoyed all the traditional pleasures of a king of France—the hunt, mistresses, court life—as well as his overriding passion: the long, weary, and monotonous practice of government.

Although clearly the leading state of Europe, the France of Louis XIV was gravely endangered by internal divisions and the excessive power that the provinces and the local nobility could wield against the centripetal strength of the monarchy. From Hugh Capet onward, the history of the French monarchy had been a constant struggle against the tendency of the French to resist royal authority. Louis XIV himself had seen his mother insulted, his soldiers attacked, and his own person subjected to humiliating control—by rebellious forces under the command of his own relatives. Louis' chief concern was to prevent recurrences of such transgressions. A characteristically royal means of achieving this end was Louis' consummate use of his court.

Because of the personalities and the troubled reigns of Louis' immediate predecessors, the court of France had been more modest in size than those of Spain or England. Louis, however, loved splendor, and he enjoyed the company of his nobles. He encouraged his

Above, Louis XIII (reigned 1610–1643). A shy, modest, and religious man, Louis XIII managed to defeat more enemies—Hapsburgs, Huguenots, nobles, and members of his own family—than perhaps any other French monarch.

nobles to come to his court, first at the Louvre and Saint-Germain, and later at the magnificent palace that grew up around his father's hunting lodge at Versailles. There, under a watchful royal eye, the courtiers were incited to compete for offices and signs of Louis' favor. Minute nuances, such as the word "For" before the names of those the king had invited to the palace of Marly or the blue jacket that the king granted to those gentlemen whom he particularly wished to honor, took on profound significance. But the responsibilities that sweetened the courtiers' life at Versailles did not extend to the exercise of power—*that* was reserved for the king and his ministers.

Versailles also served as the headquarters of the French army, which was reorganized by two of Louis XIV's ablest ministers, Michel Le Tellier and the Marquis de Louvois, his son. Structured on modern professional lines—rather than on the casual system of mercenaries that still prevailed in the rest of Europe—and led more and more by professional officers under central control, the army constituted a formidable military force. Its discipline was so legendary that the name of one of the first inspectors of the army, Lieutenant Colonel Martinet, was soon applied to any especially strict drillmaster.

But above all, at Versailles a culture and a way of life were created that set an example not only to the rest of France but also to Europe as a whole. It was a showcase for the products of French industry—particularly the tapestries and furniture in which Louis XIV took such an interest—and for the French fashions in clothes, which by 1750 dominated all Europe.

The Versailles of Louis XIV was also a center of patronage during a golden age of French literature. Louis personally intervened to protect Molière's *Tartuffe,* a damning attack on religious hypocrisy, from the reprisals of the Church. The great moralist Jean de La Bruyère, knowing intimately the workings of Versailles, was able to denounce the double dealings and viciousness of court life from his own experience.

Left, Anne of Austria, wife of Louis XIII. Facing page, above, the southwest wing of the Louvre's Cour Carrée, designed by Pierre Lescot. Facing page, below, three men who helped increase the power and authority of the Crown during the reign of Louis XIII (left to right): Pierre Séguier, the chancellor of France; Louis II of Condé (the Great Condé), victor over the Spaniards at the battle of Rocroi in 1643; and Cardinal Richelieu, Louis' chief minister.

Left, a panoramic view of the 1627 siege of La Rochelle, an important port and the principal Huguenot fortress in France. The conquest of this city was one of Cardinal Richelieu's greatest triumphs. Above, the Lantern Tower in La Rochelle. Below left, the portico of the Hôtel de Ville. Below, two towers in La Rochelle.

Jacques Bénigne Bossuet was not only a brilliant preacher but also the tutor of the dauphin, for whom he composed the *Discours sur l'histoire universelle* (1681), a classically conventional account of history beginning with God's creation of man and culminating in the triumph of a divinely ordained monarchy in Europe. Jean Baptiste Racine, perhaps the foremost playwright of the seventeenth century, was also royal historiographer of France. One of his finest plays, *Esther*, glorified Madame de Maintenon's triumph over Madame de Montespan in the battle for Louis XIV's love.

Even at the height of Louis XIV's glory, many writers and thinkers were critical of royal policies. Madame de Sévigné, for example, was on the fringe of a small group of Parisian intellectuals whom Louis XIV distrusted and feared. Racine, though a favorite of the king, infuriated Louis by daring to express disapproval of the burdens that France's wars were placing on the French populace. François de Salignac de la Mothe-Fénelon, a preacher who was appointed tutor to Louis XIV's grandsons, was in 1697 banished to his diocese of Cambrai for criticizing the king. There he wrote *Télémaque*, a moral tale intended to instruct its readers in the purpose of kingship. When it was reissued in 1717, its denunciations of war and absolutism, its praise of aristocratic liberties and the

Above, Louis XIII leading his troops through an Alpine pass between France and Italy. Under Richelieu, France fought the Hapsburgs in Italy, Spain, and the Low Countries. Following pages, the Louvre, the king's principal residence, as seen from the Pont Neuf at the time of Louis XIV (reigned 1643–1715).

States-General, and its reminder that princes were meant to work for their subjects' benefit had a profound impact on the attitudes of the eighteenth-century French elite.

The construction of royal residences, the running of the court, the launching of a vast fleet, and the maintenance of an army unmatched in size since the times of ancient Rome were all extremely expensive. Louis entrusted his finances to Jean Baptiste Colbert, a man of humble origins who rose to become the linchpin of Louis' government, supervising the economy, the navy, the colonies, and the royal building program. Largely because of Colbert, France had a relatively efficient administration during the first half of Louis' reign.

On this compact and generally well-organized country, equipped with an effective army, Louis imprinted a dynamic and bellicose foreign policy. His

Left, the Loire River near Gien. The mild climate and the nearby forests made this area extremely attractive to successive kings of France. Below, the chateau of Chantilly in the Île-de-France region of north-central France, one of the magnificent chateaux built outside the Loire Valley. Chantilly was the principal residence of the head of the Montmorency family until 1632.

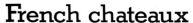

French chateaux

English victories in the north of France during the fifteenth century made the Loire Valley seem a safer place for the king of France to live than the Paris region. Up until the seventeenth century, each king spent long periods of time there: Charles VII at Chinon, Louis XI at Plessis, Louis XII at Blois, and Francis I at Chambord.

The Loire Valley developed into a political and economic center, where the States-General met and where the *livre tournois,* which soon became the currency accepted throughout France, was minted. The royal chateaux, as well as those built in the region by successful courtiers and nobles, form one of the most impressive testimonies to the splendor of royal France. Although Chinon, Plessis, and other early chateaux were essentially fortresses, guarded by hundreds of troops and rows of walls, the later royal residences, such as Blois and Chambord, presented a less military appearance.

Left, the chateau of Chambord, built by Francis I. The chateau, which has 430 rooms and 13 staircases, is surrounded by an enormous forest that is ideal for hunting. It was last used as a royal residence by Louis XIV in the 1660s. Above, the famous spiral staircase at Chambord. Much of the architectural detail of the Loire Valley chateaux remained Gothic in inspiration.

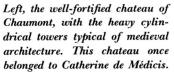

Left, the well-fortified chateau of Chaumont, with the heavy cylindrical towers typical of medieval architecture. This chateau once belonged to Catherine de Médicis.

Below, Azay-le-Rideau, built in the early sixteenth century for a royal treasurer.

Above left, Cardinal Jules Mazarin, the Italian prelate who succeeded Cardinal Richelieu as prime minister of France in 1642. Left, Jean Baptiste Colbert, the reformist finance minister of Louis XIV, who tried to moderate his sovereign's love of war and passion for Versailles. Above, Marie-Thérèse of Austria, Louis XIV's Spanish wife, with the dauphin, Louis. Shy and stupid, she proved a dull companion for her intelligent husband.

Right, Louis XIV (reigned 1643–1715). Although the French monarchy reached its greatest heights under Louis, Frenchmen suffered appallingly because of the frequent wars waged during his reign.

character, as well as the spirit of the age, which worshiped military success, made this inevitable. Louis fought against Spain, in defense of his wife's presumed rights over certain parts of its empire, and against Holland, whose independence and commercial strength annoyed him. By 1689, France found itself at war with practically the whole of Europe—the Hapsburgs and most German princes, as well as Spain and England. The conflict brought France, which had already been weakened by the revocation of the Edict of Nantes in 1685 and the subsequent expulsion of the Huguenots, to the verge of collapse.

Louis XIV's obsession with his role as a war leader

negated much of the beneficial effects of Colbert's earlier reforms. The peasants, whose lot had slightly improved in the 1660s, suffered appallingly. (In 1693 and 1694 bad harvests killed off perhaps as much as ten percent of the population.) But in 1702, France entered yet another war. The king felt that the crown of Spain, which the last of the Spanish Hapsburgs had bequeathed to Louis XIV's grandson, could not be refused: It was a crown that gave sovereignty over Spain itself, the Spanish Empire in America, the states of Milan and Naples, and the Spanish Netherlands (present-day Belgium). Europe, however, would not allow such power to pass into the hands of

Left, the interior of a printer's shop. Below, the Seine at Paris, with the palace of the Louvre on the left and the towers of Sainte-Chapelle and Notre Dame in the background on the right. Above, the bread and poultry market on the Quai des Grands-Augustins.

Bottom left, the Rue Saint-Antoine in Paris. Bottom right, the Paris fish-market.

Trade in Louis XIV's Paris

Under Louis XIV, economic activity was strictly controlled by Jean-Baptiste Colbert, the minister of finance. One of Colbert's key ideas was that a fixed amount of wealth existed in the world, so that if one state wanted to become rich it was required to subtract resources from others. Such a belief required tight government supervision of economic life at home and an economic war abroad, one aimed especially at Louis XIV's hated rivals, the Dutch. Colbert encouraged the production and export of luxury goods, such as furniture, glass, clothes, and perfumes, and worked for the creation of a colonial empire functioning in the interests of the mother country.

Above, fishermen's boats and washerwomen along the Seine in Paris. Paris was, and still is, an important river port. Right, a Paris playing-card factory. Although Louis XIV and Colbert encouraged the founding of factories, France's commercial and industrial development was impeded by the constant warfare during Louis' reign and by the revocation of the Edict of Nantes in 1685, which drove away many highly skilled Huguenot craftsmen.

Left, the admiral of France visiting the royal shipyard at Marseille. Colbert, who served as minister for the navy, strengthened the French fleet to the point where it was occasionally able to defeat the English and Dutch fleets. After Colbert's death in 1683, however, the navy declined, and it was not until the reign of Louis XVI that the French navy was again capable of challenging the English.

the Bourbons. The resulting conflict—fought in India, America, Italy, Spain, Germany, and Flanders, as well as on the high seas—has been called the first world war in history.

Historians have generally viewed this conflict, known as the War of the Spanish Succession, as a crucial ingredient in any assessment of Louis' foreign policy. Some believe that Louis had long structured his dealings with the powers of Europe around the issue of the Spanish inheritance, while others maintain that the arrogant Louis was simply borne away by overconfidence when the prospect of a dramatic increase in French territory presented itself. Which-

ever analysis is correct, it is clear that Louis' ambitions were soon shattered on the battlefield by the duke of Marlborough, the leading general of the forces opposing France, and Prince Eugene of Savoy.

The war proved disastrous for Louis and his subjects. France's armies were defeated, its coffers emptied, and its people made to suffer horribly. Yet Louis held firm until 1713, when he achieved an honorable peace. Most of the major conquests of his reign, which gave France roughly the frontiers it has today, were preserved, and his grandson remained king of Spain.

The country Louis XIV left to his great-grandson, Louis XV, no longer dominated Europe politically.

Left, the Marquise de Montespan, who became Louis XIV's mistress in 1667. Below left, the Duchesse Vallière, Louis XIV's first important mistress, who retired to a convent after the rise of the Marquise de Montespan. Below, the Marquise de Maintenon, morganatic wife of the king for the last thirty years of his life. She was the only woman to exercise some influence on Louis XIV's decisions. Right, the Hameau de la Reine at Versailles.

But it was, in the most flattering sense, the "imperial" power of Europe, for almost all the European elite used its language and copied its court, customs, and fashions. France had replaced Italy as the cultural center of Europe, in part because of royal patronage of the arts. The splendor and grandeur of Louis' Versailles encouraged other monarchs to build the magnificent palaces that can still be seen outside Vienna, Berlin, London, and Madrid—at Schönbrunn, Potsdam, Hampton Court, and Aranjuez.

In 1715, for the third consecutive time, the reign of a Bourbon began with a regency. Louis XIV's heir was a child of five, his great-grandson and the only legitimate survivor in France of numerous progeny. The regent was the duke of Orléans, Louis XIV's nephew, whose scandalous debauches had shocked his uncle. Few of the regent's internal reforms were successful. The treasury was empty, and to fill it took a lot more than the ingenious expedients of John Law. Law, the Scottish-born director-general of finances, provoked one of the most spectacular crashes in economic history in 1720 through the overissue of paper currency.

But after the death of the regent in 1723, it appeared as if the reign of Louis XV might rival in glory

Above, the entrance gate and the cour d'honneur at Versailles. Versailles contained not only the king's private and state apartments but also a chapel (the tall building on the right), apartments for all the king's relations and many of his courtiers, the offices of some of his ministers, and the barracks of his household troops.

Left, the signing of a treaty of alliance between France and the Swiss cantons in 1663. Note that Louis XIV is the only person wearing a hat—an indication of his unique status as king.

Jean de La Bruyère, one of the many writers and artists who made the reign of Louis XIV le grand siècle.

Jacques Bénigne Bossuet, bishop of Meaux, a renowned preacher and orator who served as the dauphin's tutor.

The Marquise de Sévigné, whose letters to her daughter provide an incomparable picture of life under Louis XIV.

Jean Baptiste Racine, a dramatist of genius who also wrote a number of prose works in praise of Louis XIV.

Jean de La Fontaine, who achieved lasting fame as the author of light but penetrating fables.

Molière, a playwright whose works were admired by Louis XIV and often first performed at court.

Blaise Pascal, the brilliant philosopher who gave the highest expression to French piety of the seventeenth century.

Nicolas Boileau, a critic and poet whose L'Art poétique established the principles of French classicism.

Montesquieu, who influenced both European and American political thought through his L'Esprit des lois.

Nicolas de Malebranche, a brilliant philosopher, metaphysician, and Roman Catholic theologian.

Isaac Louis Lemaistre de Sacy, a writer who won a significant place in the great flowering of talent under Louis XIV.

Above, Louis XIV during a visit to the Académie des Sciences. The king and his ministers patronized both foreign and French artists, writers, scien- *tists, and researchers. Louis' finance minister, Colbert (wearing a cross), is seen at the king's right.*

that of Louis XIV. Advised by the astute Cardinal André Hercule de Fleury, Louis appeared to be on the verge of leading France to a political hegemony in Europe that would complement its cultural domination. But the French army was faced with the excellent professional armies of Austria and Prussia, as well as those of England—a formidable power whose commercial and colonial interests were in direct conflict with those of France. Despite many expensive wars after 1733, Louis XV added only the provinces of Corsica and Lorraine to his kingdom.

Inside France the Crown continued to extend its control. The intendants—the officials first sent to the provinces by Richelieu—now became, on occasion, truly effective agents of the central government. Famines were now usually prevented by better agricultural methods, improved communications, and government intervention, although the fear of mass starvation was still ever-present. The road system, built by the government primarily to link military centers, was the best in Europe. Trade flourished as never before, and the striking eighteenth-century architecture still visible in Nantes, Bordeaux, and other port cities recalls the prosperous years of Louis XV's reign. During this period, Paris replaced Lyon as the financial capital of France.

It was during the first half of the reign of Louis XV that France's scattered colonies in North America, the West Indies, Africa, and the Indian Ocean began to develop into something that can be called a colonial empire. Hitherto their history had revealed, above all, the failings of successive French rulers: the haphazard endeavors to create an empire under Henry IV, the overambitious efforts to extend French Catholicism and the territory of the French Crown under Cardinal Richelieu, and the overregimented attempts to encourage French trade under Colbert.

The prosperity enjoyed by the Dutch in the seventeenth century fostered the conviction that colonies and overseas trade were necessary for national greatness. The Dutch, by building up the largest navy and merchant fleet in the world, had achieved an international status clearly disproportionate to the population and geographic size of the Dutch Republic. An increase in foreign commerce, and especially an expansion of trade with colonies, brought an influx of additional wealth to the Dutch; this wealth, when taxed, increased the government's revenues and enhanced its military potential and political strength. The growing influence of a commercially powerful England at the time of Louis XV's accession appeared to confirm the Dutch experience.

By its geographical position France was naturally favored for overseas expansion, perhaps even more than England. It had an extremely long Atlantic seaboard and the largest population in Europe, much of which lived on the coast and in the port cities of Rouen, Saint-Malo, Nantes, La Rochelle, and Bordeaux. Under Louis XIV, France had the essential prerequisite of foreign growth—a strong navy. During his reign, France frustrated English attempts to seize French Canada and obtained colonies in the West Indies and the Indian Ocean. In 1682, Sieur de La Salle's expedition down the Mississippi paved the way for French control of territory stretching from the Gulf of St. Lawrence to the Gulf of Mexico.

After the end of the War of the Spanish Succession in 1713, the French colonies began to assume increased importance. The trading companies founded by Colbert were reorganized by Law, and thereafter they provided a real stimulus to French commerce. By 1750 the French colonies in the West Indies and North America accounted for perhaps twenty-five percent of French overseas trade and had helped to launch an economic boom in many French ports. Saint-Malo thrived on the fishing provided by the North Atlantic and the Gulf of St. Lawrence. La Rochelle became an entrepôt for the fur trade, the most important economic activity of the French possessions in Quebec and around the Great Lakes. Nantes was a hub of the coffee trade, and Bordeaux became the distributing center for sugar from the French West Indies.

Colonial expansion continued during the reign of Louis XV. After the founding of New Orleans—named in honor of Louis' regent, the duke of Orléans—in 1718, construction began on a chain of forts linking the colonies of Louisiana and Canada. The whole central basin of North America, theoretically under the control of the king of France, blocked the westward advance of the English colonies on the Atlantic coast.

But by 1763 this French colonial empire had collapsed, largely because France was much more interested in extending its influence in Europe than in making conquests in North America or India. Moreover, the aggressively Catholic policy pursued by the Crown overseas denied the underpopulated French colonies that reservoir of heretical colonizers which

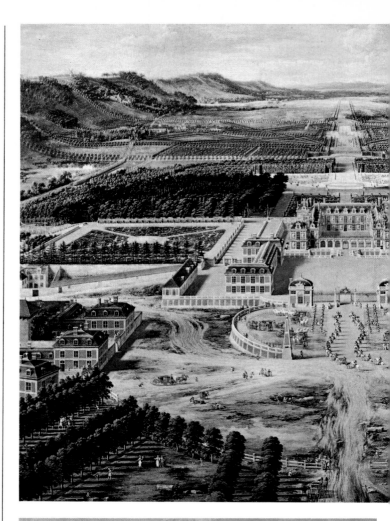

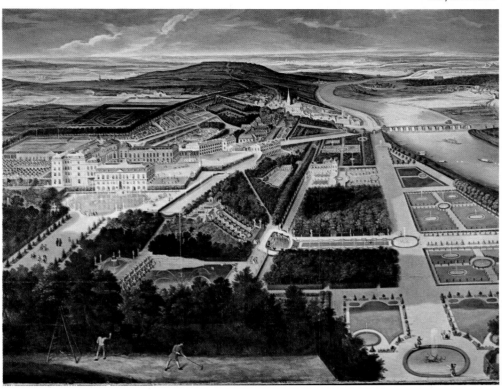

Left, the palace of Versailles in 1668, before the construction of side wings. Versailles allowed Louis XIV to engage in all his favorite country pursuits, including hunting.

Above, the palace of Saint-Cloud, the residence of Monsieur, Louis XIV's younger brother. The brother and cousins of the king of France lived far more splendidly than most European monarchs.

Left, Marly, a relatively small house a short distance from Versailles. Louis XIV would come here in the company of a few favored courtiers and relations to escape the relentlessly public routine of Versailles. The courtiers stayed in the small houses facing the lake. Marly was completely destroyed after the Revolution.

Right, Versailles in 1722. Versailles was regarded by most Frenchmen as a suitably splendid setting for the French monarchy, away from the distractions of Paris.

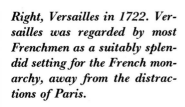

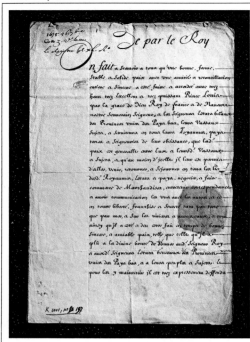

Left, Louis XIV's announcement of the Treaty of Nijmegan (1678), which ceded the old Burgundian province of Franche-Comté and some towns in Flanders to France. Below, the king's ordonnance for the publication of the Treaty of Rijswijk (1697) with England and Holland. The pact deprived Louis of some of his most recent conquests.

Louis XIV

The theoretical foundation of Louis XIV's reign is expressed in the famous statement attributed to the king: *L'état, c'est moi* ("I am the state"). The king was not only the source of legislative power but also the head of the armed forces, the first gentleman of France, and the physical embodiment of the kingdom (his children and grandchildren were called "children of France"). Nevertheless, Louis' officials were often prepared to declare royal orders unworkable or to disobey them outright. Thus Louis XIV's "absolute" monarchy was never absolutely in control of France.

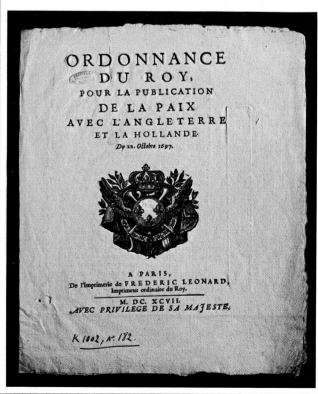

was so crucial to the success of the English colonies.

Although most of its foreign possessions had been lost, France still retained many sugar-producing islands in the West Indies, including Haiti. In the 1770s and 1780s there was a revival of French interest in overseas trade and colonies, with France recovering Saint Lucia, Tobago, and Senegal and the French Atlantic trade growing more prosperous than ever. A quarter of the West African slave trade was in French hands, and Haiti, with thirty-five thousand whites and five hundred thousand blacks, developed into one of the richest and most productive territories in the world. Louis XVI sent more French troops to Senegal, mandated a more aggressive policy in India, and dispatched the Comte de la Pérouse on a famous voyage around the world.

French overseas expansion was cut short by the Revolution, and a number of possessions were lost to England in the 1790s. French culture, however, proved a lasting force in France's former colonies. In areas as widely separated as Mauritius and Quebec, the French language is still in use today.

From the mid-eighteenth century certain sections of the French public were becoming profoundly reformist in opinion. Many of the figures involved in the movement called the Enlightenment—which sought to bring the light of reason to bear on the traditions and superstitions of society—argued for the abolition of privileges, internal customs duties, and feudal servitude, as well as the elimination of torture, the death penalty, and other vestiges of the darker past. Their idols were Reason, Progress, and Technology, and their ideal was the "Enlightened Despot"—an absolute but reforming ruler who would put their concepts into practice.

These ideas gained an increasingly important following. The *Encyclopédie* of Denis Diderot and Jean Le Rond d'Alembert, a monument to the thought of the Enlightenment, was one of the great publishing successes of the eighteenth century. Voltaire, the most brilliant, ascerbic, and popular representative of the Enlightenment, was celebrated throughout Europe; the king of Prussia declared himself not his equal but his inferior, and the czarina of Russia swore by his works.

Other writers also formed part of what was known as the *philosophe* movement. The philosophes were able to publish their works with some freedom, particularly when Chrétien Guillaume de Lamoignon de Malesherbes, a leading member of the Paris Parlement, served as chief censor in the 1750s and 1760s. Typical of the philosophes in his reliance on reason and knowledge rather than revelation and tradition

Immediately below, the fort of Mont Dauphiné, one of the many fortifications built along French frontiers by the great engineer Sébastien Le Prestre de Vauban.

Right, the Vicomte de Turenne, marshal of France and one of the most competent generals of Louis XIV's reign. Reared as a Huguenot, he was persuaded to convert to Catholicism by the king himself. Center right, the duke of Belle-Isle, who joined the army during the reign of Louis XIV and became one of the few successful generals of Louis XV's times. Bottom, the battle of Fleurus (1690), in which the French cavalry defeated a combined English, Spanish, and Imperial force.

Left, Philippe, duke of Orléans, with the young Louis XV, for whom he was regent from 1715 to 1723. Right, the crown used at the coronation of Louis XV (reigned 1715–1774). Below, Louis XV in procession to the cathedral at Reims, escorted by regiments of household troops.

was the Marquis de Condorcet, whose posthumous *Esquisse d'un tableau historique du progrès de l'esprit humain* (1794) espoused a view of history completely different from Bossuet's.

The philosophes, although they approached French society and traditions in a new and more skeptical way, were in no way political revolutionaries, and they were all extremely eager to be absorbed into the Parisian elite. Many received pensions or sinecures from the king, and by the 1770s the philosophes dominated that pillar of the status quo, the Académie Française. No one was more eager to win court favor, to cultivate courtiers, or to praise the benefits of enlightened absolutism than Voltaire. Even Jean Jacques Rousseau, who is often thought to have been a radical writer, was in practical politics conservative.

The philosophe most directly influential in politics was Montesquieu, whose *L'Esprit des lois* (1747) advocated a separation of executive, legislative, and judicial powers that was to be enshrined in the American Constitution. In its understanding of the relationships between social, climatic, political, geographic, religious, and emotional forces, *L'Esprit des lois* is one of the starting points of modern sociology.

In economics, a school of thought developed that is

Above, Marie Leczinska, daughter of King Stanislas of Poland. Marie, who married Louis XV in 1725, ceased to have any influence over her husband by 1740 and subsequently spent much of her time in the company of a few close friends.

Right, Louis XV. This portrayal in armor reflects the increasingly archaic image of the French monarchy: Most other European monarchs of this period wore military dress. Despite many defeats on the battlefield, France under Louis XV became a more prosperous, civilized, and unified kingdom.

widely held to be the first scientific school of political economy. Founded by François Quesnay, court physician to Louis XV, the "physiocrats" proceeded from the assumption that all wealth derived from agriculture. They argued for the imposition of a single tax on land to replace all the taxes that burdened the French economy and proposed the elimination of all governmental restrictions on both internal and external trade. Their famous dictum *laissez faire, laissez passer* ("let it be, let it go") succinctly expressed their conviction that natural economic laws should be allowed to prevail.

The substance of the physiocrats' theories and the doctrinaire manner in which these ideas were set forth provoked heated opposition. Nonetheless, educated circles both in France and elsewhere accepted at least some of the physiocrats' notions and greeted with approval the attempt to consider economic matters in the light of reason rather than on the basis of established custom. An economist of the time who was greatly influenced by the physiocrats, the Scot Adam Smith, wrote confidently that their system, "with all its imperfections, is perhaps the nearest approximation to truth that has yet been published on the subject."

The Enlightenment exerted a notable influence on

Right, a lit de justice *ceremony in the Paris Parlement in 1723: Louis XV (in the corner of the room, wearing a hat) is seen compelling the Parlement to register a royal edict. Through the lit de justice a king could have a measure declared law against the wishes of the Parlement.*

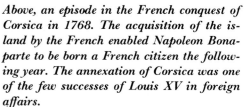

Above, an episode in the French conquest of Corsica in 1768. The acquisition of the island by the French enabled Napoleon Bonaparte to be born a French citizen the following year. The annexation of Corsica was one of the few successes of Louis XV in foreign affairs.

Near right, Madame du Barry, one of the mistresses who influenced both the life and the politics of Louis XV. Frenchmen were profoundly shocked that Madame du Barry came from a humble background and had been a Paris prostitute. Far right, Madame de Pompadour, the most celebrated of Louis XV's mistresses. A dedicated patron of the arts, she was instrumental in the founding of the royal porcelain factory at Sèvres in 1745.

Above, Louis XV at the battle of Fontenoy (1745), the last great military victory of royal France. Below, a review of a company of musketeers. The musketeers, part of the king's personal guard, were disbanded by Louis XVI in 1775.

education in France. Pointing to the need for a critically thinking citizenry, the philosophes stressed the role of state education in the development of the individual. Condorcet, a leading advocate of reform, proposed a uniform and egalitarian system of public education and set as the goal of education "the general, gradually increasing perfection of man." Overall, the Enlightenment witnessed a fundamental change in pedagogic orientation: Education came to be viewed less as a means of inculcating accepted cultural and thought patterns and more as a means of cultivating the talents of youth.

Advances in book production and an increase in literacy during the Enlightenment led to a dramatic rise in the number of books being published. It has been estimated that the amount of knowledge available in print at the end of the eighteenth century was ten times greater than that available at the end of the seventeenth century. Partly to meet the demands of this ever-expanding market, immense quantities of libelous or pornographic pamphlets attacking promi-

nent figures of church and state were produced after 1770 by people known as *Rousseaus du ruisseau* ("Rousseaus of the gutter")—many of whom were to become leaders of the French Revolution. Coupled with this phenomenon was the progressive de-Christianization of Paris, resulting to some extent from the philosophes' attacks on clericalism. In this way, one of the foundations of absolute monarchy—respect for the king and organized religion—began to lose public support.

The French monarchy, however, was still very much part of that traditional world it had already transformed to ensure its own survival. The intermittent reforming impulses of Louis XV were too often weakened by his desire to avoid conflicts with the Parlements and by pressure from vested interests at court.

In 1751 an alliance between sections of the privileged orders—the nobility and the clergy—managed to block the reforms suggested by the finance minister, Jean Baptiste Machault d'Arnouville, to revive

The Enlightenment and the *Encyclopédie*

The first half of the reign of Louis XV witnessed the triumph of the spirit of rational inquiry that had begun to pervade French life during the age of Louis XIV. The most famous and prolific writer of Louis XV's time was Voltaire. Rational and anticlerical, his books are filled with a spirit of humanity and skepticism that distinguished them from the traditional works of authors such as Jacques Bénigne Bossuet.

Voltaire also contributed to the *Encyclopédie,* one of the most important ventures of the rationalist movement of the eighteenth century—a movement today known as the Enlightenment. Edited by Denis Diderot and Jean Le Rond d'Alembert, the *Encyclopédie* was issued, despite many difficulties with the censorship, between 1751 and 1777. Its articles were planned to gather all useful knowledge, both practical and theoretical, in an easily consulted form. Although it contained many inaccuracies—Voltaire called it a mixture of wood and marble—the *Encyclopédie* was thought to be a masterpiece of modern culture and became one of the greatest publishing successes of the century.

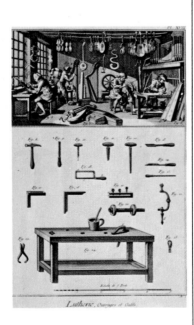

Top left, a bust of Jean Jacques Rousseau, a misanthropic thinker and writer who greatly affected educational practices of the late eighteenth century and began the revolt against the rationalism of the Enlightenment. Immediately above, the Marquis de Condorcet, a scientist who wrote an influential laudatory biography of Voltaire. The writers of the Enlightenment were very much a mutual admiration society.

Top center, Jean Le Rond d'Alembert, a brilliant mathematician who coedited the Encyclopédie *with Denis Diderot (immediately above). Right, three illustrations from the* Encyclopédie *(top to bottom): a windmill, a lute maker's shop, and pottery making. Great attention was paid to the technical and practical entries in the* Encyclopédie. *Eleven volumes of explanatory plates accompanied seventeen volumes of text in the original edition.*

Above, the opening of the States-General at Versailles in May 1789.

Left, Louis XVI (reigned 1774–1792) in his coronation robes. Unlike medieval kings, Bourbon monarchs wore royal dress only at their coronations. Near right, the 1770 marriage of Louis XVI (dauphin at the time) and Marie Antoinette of Austria. Center, Marie Antoinette in her bedroom at Versailles. The queen's ambition, extravagance, and devotion to Austrian interests lessened the prestige of the monarchy.

the economy of the country. The regime subsequently began to lose the support of the intellectuals, and the Parlements, which gave the privileged elites the best institutional means of self-expression, provided centers of opposition. Indeed, Robert François Damiens, a former servant of a Parlementaire official, was so inflamed by the conversations he heard that he tried to kill Louis XV in 1757. Public opinion—that is, the opinion of the educated minority in France—was becoming a force critical of the king. France was no longer an absolute monarchy but—as Sébastien Roch Nicolas Chamfort, a hero of the Paris salons, said—"an absolute monarchy limited by songs."

At first, Louis XV had been a devoted husband to his Polish wife, Marie Leczinska. But after she refused him her bed once too often, he began to take mistresses, including Madame de Pompadour and Madame du Barry. Both mistresses inspired a flood of hostile and contemptuous pamphlets. The court came to be regarded as a center of corruption and extravagance instead of as a shrine of royal power and splendor. Louis, who as a youth was called *le bien-aimé* ("the well-beloved"), began to lose the respect of many of his subjects. His funeral procession in 1774 was greeted with the cynical exclamation *voilà le plaisir des dames!* ("there goes the lady-killer!").

Immediately below, the Swiss financier Jacques Necker, the director of French finances from 1776 to 1781 and from 1788 to 1790. Lower right, a gold coin issued under Louis XVI. The many reforms of Louis XVI's reign alienated the nobility and the Church, traditional allies of the Crown. Nevertheless, Louis XVI remained extremely popular among his subjects until at least 1790.

The accession of Louis XVI, Louis XV's grandson, revitalized the monarchy. This simple, sober, and intelligent young man of twenty was received with religious fervor and hope at his coronation at Reims in 1775. By the 1780s, however, the court had recovered its reputation as a center of intrigue and corruption, largely because of the gossip generated by the activities of Louis XVI's ambitious and unpopular Austrian wife, Marie Antoinette. Moreover, the Crown was threatened by increasingly grave financial problems. None of the kings had managed to rationalize the tax system, which was inefficient and penalized the poor much more than the clergy, the nobility, and

the richer members of the Third Estate (bourgeoisie). Despite the ever-widening gap between the Crown's income and expenditures, Louis embarked on an extremely costly war with England in 1777. The conflict proved very useful for the American colonies in their struggle for independence, but it sharply increased the French Crown's debts.

Louis XVI's domestic reforms affected many areas of national life. The army was increased in size and its weaponry and engineers were recognized to be the best in Europe. Provincial assemblies were founded. Torture was abolished and the Huguenots recovered a few basic human rights, much to the horror of the

Above, the return of the king to Paris from Versailles in October 1789. Immediately below, supporters of Louis XVI being disarmed, on the king's orders, at the Tuileries palace in February 1791. Bottom, the arrest of the king after his attempt to flee Paris in June 1791.

The French Revolution

The French Revolution destroyed first the traditional monarchy (1789–1791), then the new constitutional monarchy (1792), and finally the monarch himself (1793). Yet, as the historian Alexis de Tocqueville pointed out, it also realized many of the traditional ambitions of royal France's rulers. The National Assembly of 1789–1791 gave France at long last a uniform and relatively efficient administrative system, and the abolition of the privileges of the Church and the nobility in 1789 greatly increased the power of the central government, especially to raise taxes.

It was by no means inevitable that the Revolution would lead to the proclamation of a republic. Louis XVI had shown that he was prepared to abandon the absolute powers of his ancestors by calling a meeting of the States-General in May 1789. But Frenchmen doubted the sincerity of Louis XVI's acceptance of the constitutional monarchy of 1791–1792. In 1792 foreign armies invaded France, claiming that they came to rescue the king and his family. The popular conviction—most probably incorrect—that Louis was in alliance with the foreigners led to his imprisonment on August 13, 1792.

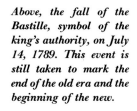

Above, the fall of the Bastille, symbol of the king's authority, on July 14, 1789. This event is still taken to mark the end of the old era and the beginning of the new.

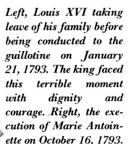

Left, Louis XVI taking leave of his family before being conducted to the guillotine on January 21, 1793. The king faced this terrible moment with dignity and courage. Right, the execution of Marie Antoinette on October 16, 1793.

Catholic Church. But by 1787 the Crown no longer had the necessary prestige to carry out radical reforms, nor would the increasingly independent and ambitious clergy and nobility cooperate. A profound gulf existed between the Crown and public opinion. Many of the poor, seeing the royal troops that guarded grain convoys, even came to believe that the court was conspiring to cause famines in order to sell grain at high prices.

In 1788, largely to avoid a declaration of bankruptcy, the king convoked the States-General—the ancient assembly of clergy, nobility, and the Third Estate—which had not met since 1614. When the body met in May 1789 at Versailles, a violent clash broke out between the majority of the Third Estate and the clergy on the one hand and the majority of the nobility on the other. It was not, essentially, a class conflict, because bourgeois nonnobles had been buying land and merging into the nobility since at least the reign of Francis I and mingling on terms of equality with nobles in Paris and provincial salons since the reign of Louis XV. It was, rather, a conflict about how power should be exercised—either through traditional institutions, like the Parlement and the States-General, or through a new, more "democratic" assembly.

Above, the attack on the Tuileries palace on August 10, 1792. This palace, the residence of Louis and his family since their forcible removal from Versailles in 1789, was defended by only a few hundred guards and nobles.

Left, the guillotining of Louis XVI. The execution, which horrified the Parisian crowd, had been ordered by an unrepresentative assembly that dared not consult the French people. Right, Maximilien François Marie Isidore de Robespierre, a ruthless leader of the Revolution, who was himself guillotined in 1794.

On June 17, leaders of the Third Estate declared themselves to be the representatives of the nation and asked the deputies of the clergy and nobility to join with them in a national assembly. Louis XVI ordered the nobility and clergy to comply with this request. At this point, however, popular fury asserted itself.

On July 14 a crowd attacked the Bastille, the great fortress-prison in the middle of Paris that stood as a grim symbol of oppression. A national guard was set up to ensure law and order and to defend the revolutionaries, and the red, white, and blue tricolor of the revolution was adopted. On August 4, in one of the most extraordinary transformation scenes in French history, the National Assembly abolished all privileges, those of towns and provinces as well as those of the clergy and nobility. It seemed as if the past itself was dead and that all Frenchmen were about to enter the new revolutionary paradise heralded by *liberté, égalité,* and *fraternité.*

But 1789 was also the year of a terrible harvest. Some began to fear that the king and the court were plotting to defeat the revolution by withholding food from the populace. On October 5 the king was seized at Versailles by a Paris mob and taken by force to that dangerous, overpopulated capital from which Louis XIV had removed the seat of government in

1682. In 1791, having failed in an attempt to flee the country, Louis decided to sign a constitution limiting his powers and swore loyalty to the nation; his credibility, however, had been seriously hurt. Most Frenchmen concluded that he was in league with the foreigners who invaded France in mid-1792. On January 21, 1793, Louis was guillotined. "I die innocent of all the crimes imputed to me," he said before the blade fell.

Louis thus paid for his rejection of the military traditions of the kings of France, who had always been war leaders first and lawgivers second. Unlike Louis XIV or Louis XV, Louis XVI had never led his army in battle; he had hardly ever even reviewed it. Unlike Henry III in 1588 or Louis XIV in 1648, Louis XVI in 1789 was unable to oppose the forces of revolution with a loyal body of troops and allowed himself to become a prisoner in Paris. In the past the king had been the vital apex of the social order, the man able (according to an old proverb) to "take everything and pay for everything" because he was strong enough and rich enough to do so. But after 1789, Louis XVI could guarantee neither the old nor the new social order. He had become dispensable, and so a monarchy founded by force was ended by force.

Nonetheless, royal France had existed for so long that it could not die overnight. Many of its attitudes and much of its political support lasted into the nineteenth century. Indeed, the Bourbons were restored in 1814 in the person of Louis XVI's brother Louis XVIII, who was succeeded by another brother and a cousin before the proclamation of the Second Republic in 1848. Even today, many officials of the Fifth Republic work in buildings and offices built for servants of the king. And the frontiers of the France of President Valéry Giscard d'Estaing are basically those left to it by his ancestor Louis XV.

Great Britain

"The past is a foreign country: they do things differently there." The contemporary English novelist L. P. Hartley might well have been writing of the British Empire, so distant it now seems. At its territorial height, between the two world wars, the British Empire extended into every continent of the globe. In 1947, when the sunset of the empire began with independence in Asia—with India, Pakistan, and Ceylon achieving their sovereignty at midnight on August 15—the British flag flew over 900 million people. From that empire would spring fifty new nations. No empire has ever been so vast, has governed so large a

population, has spawned so many national identities.

All empires are a combination of the glorious and the tawdry, of uplifting change and of grinding oppression. The British were convinced, as their empire grew, that they held in trust the lives of millions of people to whom they were transferring the benefits of civilization as they defined it: high technology, in the form of improved sanitation, transportation, and communication; the advantages of an English-style education; moral regeneration, through the work of the many missionary groups that went out from London, Canterbury, York, Durham, and Edinburgh; a common language of trade, English; and perhaps

Preceding page, the Royal Arms of Great Britain, on the back of the throne in the House of Lords, designed in Gothic style in the early nineteenth century by A. W. Pugin. This page, top, sheep country—the Marlborough Downs, in Wiltshire. Center left, Land's End, Cornwall, the westernmost point in England. Land's End looks out on the Atlantic Ocean, in the age of sail the sea bridge to an empire. Center right, a partial view of the seven chalk cliffs on the south coast of England, known as the Seven Sisters. Above left, the White Cliffs of Dover, facing France.

Near left, the Wye River Valley in Herefordshire, on the Welsh border. The Border Marches, about 150 miles from London, marked the traditional boundary between England and Wales. Above, sheep pastures on the Black Mountains in Wales.

On Scotland's windswept Culloden Moor (above), on April 16, 1746, the troops of England's King George II decimated the army of Charles Edward Stuart, Bonnie Prince Charlie, pretender to the English throne. The battle confirmed English power even in the Scottish Highlands. Below, the mountain barrier of the Border Lands that sets Scotland apart from England.

above all, an evenhanded system of justice by one's peers.

Within the empire many of the "native subjects" were genuinely grateful it was England and not another nation that was spurring their modernization. In colonies of settlement—in North America, Australia, and southern Africa—white settlers sought to achieve a delicate balance between continued loyalty to Britain and an emerging sense of their own separate identity. At times the balance was not achieved and revolution resulted, as in North America between 1775 and 1783. At other times, a new nation would evolve through the gradual transfer of power from the British Parliament at Westminster to new parliaments in Ottawa, Canada; Canberra, Australia; or Wellington, New Zealand.

The idea of an empire was based on an assumption of superiority. An empire builder assumed that he knew what was best, for himself, for his nation, and for the people in his charge. A nineteenth-century British commissioner in the tiny West African colony of The Gambia expressed the mixture of motives well, writing in his journal:

There are higher purposes in life than merely living. Perhaps I shall die here, but I shall die a better man for

bbacia de bello ubi tumpharat fundau. Regnau anis xvi · 7 aplui

aula Weltm gltrit. eande tagta puit frm regnauad

Willelm rer anglie pmi pco quisiconem ei

Wild rer ku

Henricus se nior rer tei annav · vo

Ster Rer

Iste henricus vir potens · 7 sapiens jurau leges sci edwardi in cl abris tene. ß frm uicar frem suu · noluit. Hobne cenobiu de Radigo ubi sepulc iac; fundau · 7 epatu gstitunt karl. Regnau an nnis xxxvi · 7 circiter dimidiu.

Iste Stephanus miles strenuissim omnib; dieh; dubus eatb; bellou ipstitut. Isto abbacam de feuerd fundauit. In qua ipe · 7 Eustachii filius ei · 7 matilda uxor ei iacent sepulti. Iste Regnauit ann s xix.

having been here. These people are degraded, ignorant, swept by disease; how low, how low they stand. Yet, they *stand.* I can help move them that inch higher, give them that direction they need, tell them of that truth that, once grasped, lived, proved, may one day make them right-thinking Englishmen, men with souls as white as any other, men I will have been proud to have known. Lift them, lift them! If I pass through the Gate before them, one day they too will pass through it, and I, there before them, will welcome them as mine.

How can one utterly condemn this amalgam of humanitarianism, purpose, drive, and sacrifice? Yet does one not condemn this amalgam of arrogance, self-righteousness, and superiority? Here, in this combination of imperialism, Christianity, racism, and technology, one finds the reasons why a tiny island nation held sway over the greatest modern empire: for God, for Glory, and yes, for Gold. Comprising a nation of traders from a green and pleasant land that was too small to contain its fermenting energies, the British reached out from the hub to the outer rim of the world. When, between 1947 and 1965, Britain effectively dismantled its colonial empire, it left behind its language, its literature, its laws, and its lessons of governance.

Even the most populous English-speaking nation in the world, the United States, cannot forget its heritage in Elizabethan, Georgian, and Victorian England. As that most American of poets, Walt Whitman, remarked, "I hear continual echoes from the Thames." Images of the rolling hills of Devon, visions of the rivers and valleys of Britain, echoes of the "White Cliffs of Dover," the plays of Shakespeare, and Yorkshire pudding—all are part of the American mythology. King Arthur and the knights of his Round Table shape the imaginations of young Americans as they have generations of Britons. Ultimately, the British Empire was an empire of the mind. The first modern nation, Britain built its empire just as Rome once built its, even on British soil. It dominated the imagination of the nineteenth century and more, setting goals others sought to imitate.

Facing page, left to right, top and bottom, the Norman kings of England: William I (the Conqueror), reigned 1066–1087; William II (Rufus, or the Red), reigned 1087–1100; Henry I (Strongbow), reigned 1100–1135, who led the first conquest of Ireland; and Stephen of Blois, reigned 1135–1154, an ineffective ruler. The figures are from Matthew Paris' chronicle of the world.

Above, King Arthur watching a dance at court. The Arthurian legend—for almost all that we know of him derives from mythology—presents an ideal world of knighthood and medieval chivalry. Right, St. John's Chapel in the Tower of London. Built for William I, the chapel typifies Norman architecture.

Bayeux tapestry

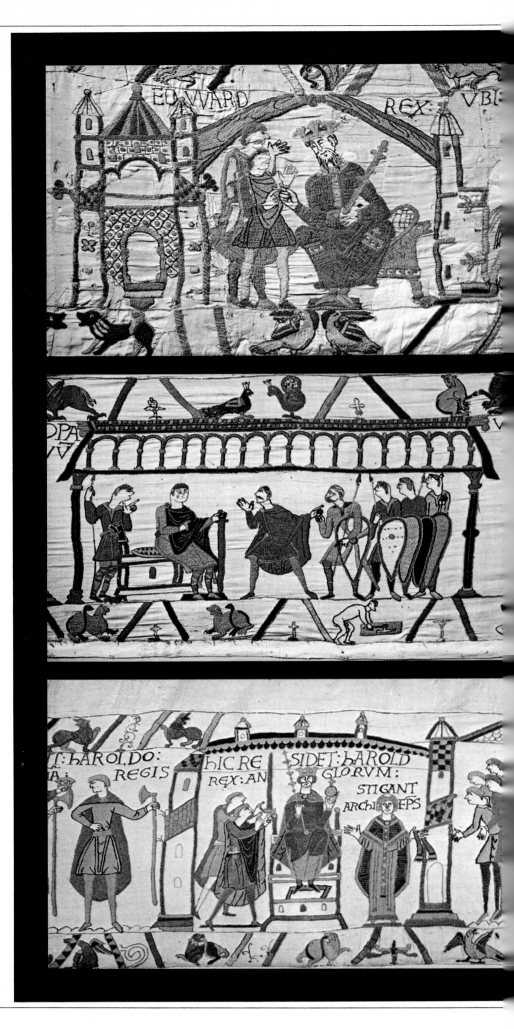

History is not always best told by documents. The most famous account of the Norman Conquest, which brought William the Conqueror to power in England in 1066, is given in a remarkable tapestry woven for public exhibition. This pictorial record—actually a coarse strip of linen, 231 feet long and 19½ inches wide—was once believed to have been embroidered by Queen Matilda, William's wife, at the request of Odo, bishop of Bayeux; it was in this French city that Harold, the future Saxon king of England, had sworn an oath of allegiance to William in 1064. While Matilda's role in the creation of this work is now doubted, the tapestry is almost certainly English and was made around 1083. Yet we know almost nothing of the work until its appearance in 1476 in the inventory of the Bayeux Cathedral's possessions, after which it disappeared, to be rediscovered by French archaeologists in the eighteenth century. The most important of its kind in the world, the tapestry now hangs safely in the Bayeux Museum in the historical region of Normandy.

The Bayeux tapestry, showing seventy-two embroidered episodes, most of them appearing in eight colors, is rich in detail, especially with respect to costumes. This page, top, Edward the Confessor, king of England (reigned 1042–1066), sending Harold, his brother-in-law and chief minister, to Normandy; center, William the Conqueror, seated, granting an audience to Harold; bottom, Harold returning to have himself crowned king in January of 1066. War soon followed, for it is believed that William may have been promised the English crown during an earlier visit with his cousin Edward. Facing page, top left, the Normans building ships for their invasion; top right, the Great Fleet crossing the English Channel. The English and French battle at Hastings (facing page, center) while Bishop Odo (not shown) cheers the Normans on. Two thousand horsemen and three thousand infantry destroyed Harold's forces. Facing page, bottom left, the English defending themselves with shields; bottom right, King Harold's death in October of 1066.

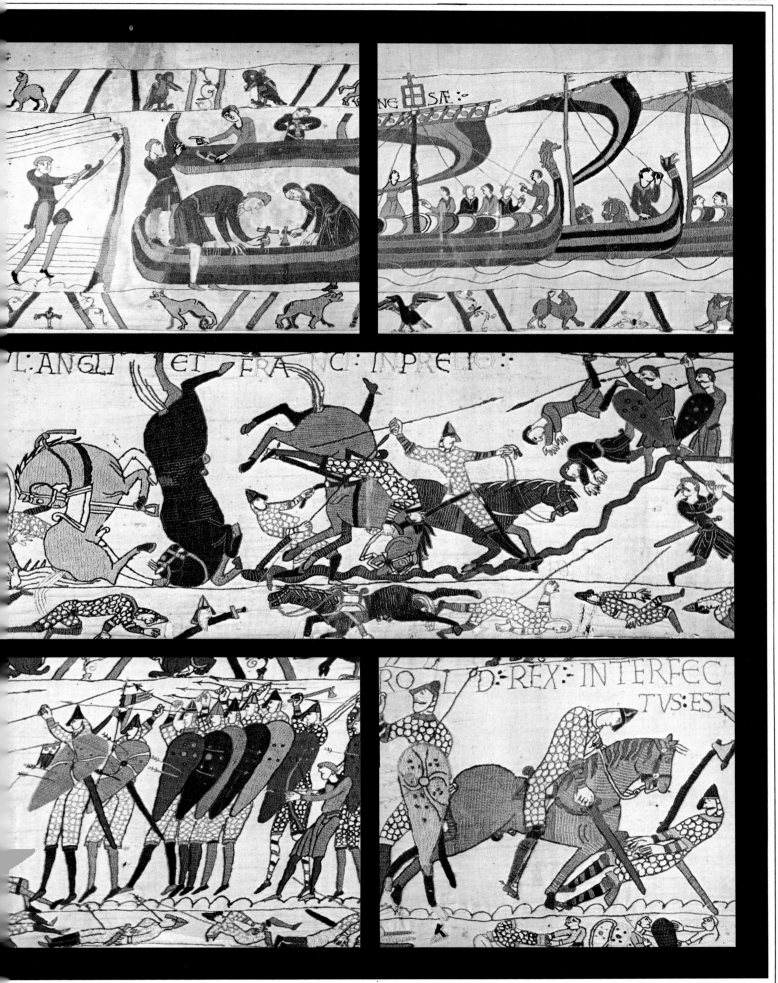

In 1170, Thomas à Becket, archbishop of Canterbury, was assassinated while at prayer (right), perhaps at the behest of Henry II. Above, a window in Canterbury Cathedral showing Henry at penance.

Construction on Canterbury Cathedral, Mother Church of England, commenced about 1070. While not the most highly acclaimed architecturally, the cathedral has been enshrined in such great literary works as The Canterbury Tales. Facing page, top left, the Bell Harry Tower of the cathedral, the most beautiful Perpendicular-Gothic structure in England. Far right, the choir of the cathedral looking east toward the altar. Facing page, below left, a gilded copper casket with Limoges enamels, said to be a reliquary of Saint Thomas. It stands in the treasury of Anagni Cathedral, near Rome. Canonized in 1173, Becket made Canterbury a place of pilgrimage.

The British Empire is said to have begun with the great age of exploration in the early sixteenth century. Together with Spain, Holland, France, and Portugal, Britain created an "imperial revolution," transforming the world through the expansion of Europe overseas. Yet one may not quite understand England in its multitude of contradictions—its democratically aristocratic way of life, its affluence and early industrial dominance, its love of monarchy and concern for the common man, its established church and its empty church halls—without a journey even further back into the novelist Hartley's "foreign country."

An island people, the English always thought in strategic terms. In a sense, the development of Britain's great overseas empire was in response to the lack of resources within the island kingdom and to the awareness that only by expanding overseas could England ever hope to be safe in the presence of larger and inherently more powerful nations. England had suffered many invasions at the hands of the Romans, Angles and Saxons, and Danes, even before the successful conquest by the Normans in 1066. Since that year, when the troops of the adventurous duke of Normandy defeated the Anglo-Saxon army of King Harold II at Hastings, and Duke William—rightly

called the Conqueror—was crowned king of England in Westminster Abbey on Christmas night, England has not been invaded by sea. Systematically, English kings pressed back the English borders, west along the Wye River into Wales and north against Emperor Hadrian's long abandoned Roman Wall to the ultimate defeat of Scotland. Crossing the sea, they conquered Ireland, and dominated this land—England's first overseas colony—until 1800, when the British Parliament voted on an act of legislative union, forming the United Kingdom of Great Britain and Ireland. Britain would prove impregnable—to the Spanish, whose great Armada sank before the British

"Protestant Winds"; to the French under Napoleon; and to the Germans under Adolf Hitler.

The Normans, originally Norsemen from Scandinavia, had been invited by the French kings in the early tenth century to settle the territory in northwest France henceforth known as Normandy. This area grew into a powerful and aggressive state whose Norman rulers eventually invaded and conquered England while still remaining vassals to the king of France. After establishing themselves in England and acquiring legal ownership of all English land in 1066, the Norman-English kings (who remained as "French" as they were "English") drew on their new

Taken captive by Duke Leopold V of Austria in 1192 as he returned from the Third Crusade, King Richard I, the Lionhearted, was imprisoned in Durnstein Castle (above) on the Danube. Once his liberty was purchased by an enormous ransom in 1194, Richard returned to England for a short time, then spent his remaining years warring with Philip II in France. Above right, Richard's Austrian capture, and his eventual submission to Holy Roman Emperor Henry VI.

wealth to become an even greater threat to the French monarchy. By involving themselves in almost continuous wars with France in an attempt to acquire and maintain additional French territory, the kings persistently menaced their neighbors across the English Channel.

The Normans remade medieval England. William the Conqueror built the Tower of London to guard the Thames as he built great, solid Norman cathedrals to guard the Church. To assure loyalty from his followers, William shared his conquest with them. He instituted a vast survey of vanquished resources—of population, land, wealth, minerals, and cattle—to determine tax assessment. This, the *Domesday Book* of 1086, both demonstrated and aided William's desire

to achieve political and administrative centralization, and thereby strengthened the power of the monarchy. By the end of his reign in 1087, William had created an Anglo-Norman state, had won the support of the Church to his ends, and—while still technically a vassal to the king of France—had set England on the path to independence. At the same time, William had drawn England into the broader world of Europe.

For a century thereafter England was governed by a series of weak kings who were unable to make peace between warring barons. Each baron—the vassal of another higher lord (either a duke or king)—was engaged in a feudal contract by which he gave allegiance and military service in exchange for a grant of land. Chaos frequently broke out during the absence of the Norman-English kings (who were preoccupied with upholding their French possessions) when their vassals, the barons, used their private armies to make war on each other or on the monarchy.

In 1100, King William II (Rufus, or the Red), son of William the Conqueror, was killed by an arrow while hunting in the royal forest. He was succeeded by his brother Henry I, who reunited Normandy—held by their eldest brother, Robert Curthose—to England, but now with the English kingdom as the chief partner. Henry also created the best-organized fiscal system in Europe and instituted a network of

Above, Winchester Cathedral, in the heart of a city that served as England's capital from Alfred the Great's ninth-century reign as Saxon king of Wessex through the time of William the Conqueror. The cathedral, the second longest in Europe, was constructed from 1079 until 1404; inside are the tombs of King Canute, the Great, and of William II. The transept (seen here) is Norman, but the cathedral blends several styles successfully.

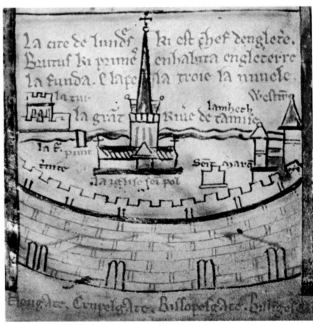

Above, the Magna Carta, signed by King John, Richard I's successor, on June 15, 1215. It is now kept in London's British Museum.

Above right, a detail from a painted stall in the sanctuary of Westminster Abbey, probably depicting Henry III, King John's son. Right, a medieval miniature by the historian Matthew Paris showing London dwarfed by the Norman cathedral of St. Paul, which was destroyed in the Great Fire of 1666.

Above, Edward II, king of England from 1307 to 1326, with his wife, Isabella of France, from a manuscript written for his son, Edward III, by Walter de Milemete. Isabella broke with Edward II and in 1325 conspired for his removal. He abdicated in favor of his son the next year, was imprisoned in Berkeley Castle, and was assassinated while in captivity. Edward II was entombed (below) in Gloucester Cathedral, under a masterpiece of Gothic funerary art.

itinerant justices who carried the royal law to the people. When he died in 1135, leaving as his only heir a daughter, Matilda, the barons refused to accept a woman's rule and crowned the indecisive Stephen of Blois, son of William the Conqueror's daughter, the new king. Contentious barons refused to accept his legitimacy, however, and the country was plunged into anarchy.

It was Stephen's successor, Henry Plantagenet, who as Henry II re-established royal power in England. Through his marriage to Eleanor of Aquitaine, former wife of the French king Louis VII, Henry gained territories in France. Through wars, diplo-

Left, the tombs of Richard II (reigned 1377–1400) and his first wife, Anne of Bohemia. It is written that Richard's devotion to his wife was so abiding that he would not allow her to leave his side. Placed in the chapel of Edward the Confessor, in Westminster Abbey, these effigies were a customary form of medieval art.

Medieval manuscripts embellished with miniature paintings often depict the everyday life of the times. Above, meat being cooked on a spit; below, state personages being transported on a pilgrimage. Both illustrations are from a codex of the fourteenth century, known as the View of London.

macy, and the marriages of his children he acquired additional lands on the Continent. England thus became embroiled in Europe's affairs. Henry's reign is celebrated for two developments: the genesis of the English common law and of the jury system. These two advances provided a uniform system of justice for all of England.

As part of his expansion of the administration of justice, Henry appointed his friend Thomas à Becket archbishop of Canterbury in an effort to exercise judicial authority over the Church. When Henry attempted to have clerics tried in royal courts, however, the archbishop would have none of it, defending the prerogatives of the Church against the king. Thus began the controversy between king and archbishop (and the French king Louis VII, who had sided with Becket) that culminated on December 29, 1170. On that fateful night, four knights—perhaps not sent by the king, but certain of his approval—killed Becket in his own cathedral. Eventually Becket would be canonized, and as Saint Thomas he became the most noted of English saints. In time Henry, disillusioned and weak, would recognize that while establishing himself as the greatest monarch in Europe he had sown the seeds of revolt within England, of continued rivalry with the Church, and of war with France.

In 1189, Henry died in the midst of domestic strife over territorial inheritances, and his eldest surviving son, having rebelled against him with the aid of the French king Philip II Augustus, ascended the throne as Richard I, the Lionhearted. Far more interested in Continental affairs than in those of his own country, Richard carried the Crusaders to the gates of Jerusalem. The Crusades, an attempt by the Church, king, and knights of Europe to reconquer the Holy Land taken by the Seljuk Turks, gave England a sense of pride, stimulated finance and commerce, and brought to the isles many new ideas from elsewhere in Europe and the East.

In 1192, upon his return from the Crusades, Richard was imprisoned by the duke of Austria. The tax imposed upon his English subjects to pay his ransom played into the hands of the barons—who were already growing in power. This situation placed the monarchy in the weak position of requesting favors of an already restless nobility. Richard's death seven years later left his brother and successor, John, of whom he had been openly contemptuous, seriously compromised. To reinforce his faltering authority, John attempted to curtail some of the traditional rights of the barons, thereby fanning open rebellion. On June 15, 1215, on the plains of Runnymede, in

Left, Henry V (reigned 1413–1422) who, as heir to the throne, was depicted by Shakespeare as Prince Hal, a drinking companion of Falstaff, and once upon the throne, as a living symbol of patriotism. Henry VI (below) was a central protagonist of the Wars of the Roses (1455–1485).

In 1453, Henry VI suffered his first serious mental illness, precipitating the Yorkist rebellion that brought the duke of York to the throne as Edward IV in 1461. In happier years, England had controlled Tournai, in Belgium, where ca. 1450, this Devonshire tapestry (below) was woven. The scenes depict a shepherdess, a cowherd, the preparation of a falcon for the hunt, two views of a boar hunt, and the sounding of the oliphant, a type of horn.

the southern county of Surrey, he submitted to the demands of his more powerful opponents—who had won the support of the Church—and signed Magna Carta (Great Charter), a statement of the rights of free Englishmen. In reviving the concept of the feudal contract—which proclaimed that rights accompanied duties between vassal and lord—the barons won from the reluctant Crown an acknowledgment of limits on royal powers.

Though conservative in its original intent, Magna Carta rightly stands as the first great document on the path to modern democracy. The charter was rooted in the principle of compromise between the

ruler and the ruled, as is democracy, and even though it confirmed only the highest rank of barons in their rights and privileges, it also contained enough that was new to justify the regard in which we hold it. From Magna Carta came the principle of *habeas corpus* (protection from arbitrary arrest); the notion that the consent of the taxpayer should be given with respect to the degree of taxation; and the precedent that citizenship should, in time, be extended to all classes. (The last would be especially important to the development of a sense of imperial responsibilities, as when, by the nineteenth century, members of the empire would be considered not only subjects of the Crown but also citizens of their own country.) The principle of checks and balances, acting as a safeguard against the absolute power of monarchs, had been struck.

Throughout the twelfth and thirteenth centuries, serfdom was giving way to a condition, first, of peasantry and, then, of a less aristocratically structured society. A middle class was emerging, and this class would seek more systematic ways of trade. Still, the Church remained the dominant force, as demonstrated by Henry III's rebuilding of Westminster Abbey in the thirteenth century. This century also saw first Oxford and then Cambridge take shape as universities. A sense of being one English nation, enhanced by the growth of parliamentary practices and the extension of one judicial system, began to override even the divisive forces of civil wars and a succession of ineffective and troubled kings.

The kings of England continued to try to expand their power. Edward I conquered north Wales in 1283; in 1314 Edward II failed miserably, at Bannockburn, to conquer Scotland; and Edward III, who came to the throne in 1327, dared to challenge the French. Claiming the French throne through his mother, as grandson of Philip IV of France, Edward instigated the long struggle between England and France known as the Hundred Years' War (1337–

In the fourteenth century, coins became increasingly important forms of exchange. Above right, a rose noble, or royal coin, depicting Edward IV, struck in 1465. Under Edward, the King's Council was brought to heel and much of its civil jurisdiction was transferred to a Court of Chancery (right), the origin of one of the great offices of state, the Office of the Chancellor. Facing page, a traditional depiction of Edward IV vanquishing the earl of Warwick at the battle of Barnet in 1471. With this defeat, Edward removed his most skillful opponent.

ez vius que noftre fouueraim
feigneur ez edward tiesfart
par la grace de dieu roy den
gleterre et de france / et feigne
du lande / departift du vais de zellande et

The Tower of London long dominated the city, as fort and as prison. Left, the duke of Orléans, imprisoned in the White Tower (1415–1440), writing poetry. Immediately below, the central tower. Bottom, the Traitors' Gate, set into St. Thomas' Tower on the banks of the Thames. Through this gate state prisoners could be taken directly from the river. Famous prisoners included Sir Thomas More, Sir Walter Raleigh, and Anne Boleyn.

1453). He also attempted to promote economic independence for England: By forbidding the exportation of raw wool and the importation of manufactured wool goods, he hoped to stimulate English trade and manufacturing. Edward's tactics were based on an early version of the theory of mercantilism, or maintenance of a favorable balance of trade. His early economic strategy later gave rise to the "circle of commerce" established in the eighteenth century, which involved supplies of raw materials from colonies, ready markets within the colonies, and the use of English vessels in which both produce and finished goods would be carried.

During Edward III's reign, the long war with France, the development of a central treasury, and the rise of the idea of the state had made heavier taxation necessary, increasing the people's already

Left, Henry VII (reigned 1485–1509), the first Tudor king. Right, nobles and their ladies going to a tournament, from the chronicles of Jean Froissart, who left vivid portrayals of fourteenth-century English life. Below, a fifteenth-century codex from the Bodleian Library, Oxford, showing the unloading of a merchant ship in The City, the financial center of London.

growing dissatisfaction with the burdens of war and the devastation to their lands and to the knightly class. While Edward was preoccupied with asserting his claims in France, the power of Parliament had grown substantially. When his successor, his young grandson Richard II, came to the throne in 1377, the parliamentarians were determined to retain their new power. Once he came of age in 1389, Richard promised to conform to the wishes of Parliament, but eight years later, feeling strong enough to challenge those who earlier had shackled him, he tried a parliamentary petitioner for treason. Imprisoning his critics without trial, Richard effectively encouraged his subjects to rise against him.

In 1399, Richard, the last Plantagenet king, was forced to abdicate the throne in favor of his cousin Henry Bolingbroke, of the House of Lancaster (this usurpation set the stage for the later Wars of the Roses, in which the legitimacy of Henry's Lancastrian line was challenged). Owing his position to the support of the Parliament, the new king, Henry IV, naturally acknowledged its ascendancy, while suppressing the rebellions of Richard's supporters.

With the Scots and the Welsh in open revolt and receiving French aid, the Hundred Years' War continued. The crown was worn by a troubled monarch, insecure until he might vanquish France on the battlefield. Nonetheless, the early years of the renewed war went well for Henry. The last Welsh defenders were finally starved out at Harlech Castle in 1409, as the French fell victim to domestic crises.

When the young Henry V came to the throne in 1413, he inherited a nearly unified nation in which English had replaced Norman French as the language

of the court and in which people were prosperous enough to sustain a foreign war. Invading France in 1415, Henry V inflicted a humiliating defeat on the French at Agincourt, and by marriage and treaty was named heir to France. The promise of an interim of peace was shattered when Henry died of dysentery while still in the field in 1422, leaving the English crown to his son Henry VI, who was less than a year old. The reign of the mentally deranged Henry sufficiently weakened the monarchy, and in 1455 a struggle for the throne, known as the Wars of the Roses, erupted, splitting the great nobility of England into two factions: the House of Lancaster (descendants of Henry IV) whose symbol was a red rose and the House of York (descendants of Edmund, duke of York) whose symbol was a white rose. By 1461, Edward of York had won the throne, becoming Edward IV.

The wars continued for almost a quarter of a century until 1485. The next year the Lancastrian Henry Tudor, who became Henry VII, united the Yorkist and Lancastrian claims through his marriage to Elizabeth of York. By this point, all contenders, French and English, Yorkist and Lancastrian, had been bled white, their economies in tatters, their social structures wobbling in the face of constant war, plagues, and taxation. Yet during this time a sense of national identity was emerging on both sides of the English Channel: It was for France that the century's prime symbol, Joan of Arc, died, and it was for England that the English armies fought. A tense dialogue between Crown and Parliament had produced the be-

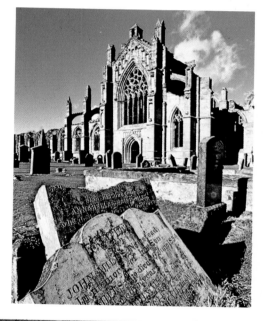

Left, a detail from court painter Hans Holbein's famed portrait of Henry VIII, capturing the king in all his strength in 1540. Above, left to right, four of Henry's wives: Catherine of Aragon as painted by Michel Sittow; Anne Boleyn; Jane Seymour; and Catherine Parr.

Above right, windows at the palace of Hampton Court, showing Henry VIII's family tree. Right, Melrose Abbey in Scotland, burned in 1545 during Henry's invasion of the north. Below left, Henry's fifth wife, Catherine Howard. Below right, Anne Boleyn's grave marker in the Royal Chapel of St. Peter, Tower of London.

Henry VIII's lord chamberlain, or chief steward, William Sandys, built The Vyne (above) at Sherborne St. John, in Hampshire. The house, begun in the early sixteenth century, is typical of the Tudor style (with neoclassical and Palladian additions); it was a common stopping place for royalty and others on the road to Winchester.

ginnings of the modern political state; English had become the medium of communication; and the "father of English poetry," Geoffrey Chaucer, had captured in *The Canterbury Tales* the sense of a nation that was on a pilgrimage to find (or to make) itself.

A new dynasty, one which would truly launch Britain in quest of an empire, came to the throne in the person of Henry VII, a Tudor whose house would rule for over a century. A colorful, vicious, romantic history was at an end. The age of the knight, of barons as kingmakers, would give way to a more centralized government, an ever-stronger Parliament, and the rise of that nation of shopkeepers upon which the middle class, and thus an empire, was founded.

The voyages of Christopher Columbus heralded the end of the Middle Ages, for soon new lands and

their products and promises would put to an end the lingering feudal structures of society in western Europe. Henry VII, who ruled from 1485 to 1509, would prove to be the first "modern" king, centralizing power, founding a new state in conscious preparation for more splendid destinies. An intelligent, despotic, pragmatic man, Henry (who always pronounced his name Harry) modernized the techniques of warfare, laid the foundations for a fleet that would become mistress of the seas, promoted commerce and exploration, brought in new taxes in more acceptable guises, and stayed on the good side of a Parliament which seldom met. He left to his son, Henry VIII, a country that had been run like a good business.

Henry VIII, sportsman, womanizer, egoist, was an imposing force of great intelligence and even greater cunning. Aided by an effective minister, Cardinal Thomas Wolsey, Henry plunged into European politics, taking first one side and then the other in the struggle between the French monarchs and the Spanish Hapsburgs for control of certain Italian territories. A Renaissance monarch, Henry governed according to the principles of Machiavelli: Self-interest (he identified himself and the state as one) was paramount, and people were used to that end or discarded. He completed the annexation of Wales

Above, an allegorical scene from the National Portrait Gallery in London showing Edward VI, who ascended the throne at ten and died at sixteen. Henry VIII, his father, lies on the bed; a book inscribed "The word of the Lord endureth forever" falls on the pope's head as an inset depicts the destruction of images. Taken together, the scene tells of the consolidation of Protestantism during Edward's reign (1547–1553); a Council of Regency— initially led by Edward's uncle, the duke of Somerset, head of the powerful Protestant Seymour family—actually ruled.

Below, Thomas Wolsey, powerful cardinal and lord chancellor under Henry VIII. Near right, the sixteenth-century English statesman and author Thomas More. Above far right, Thomas Cranmer, first Anglican archbishop of Canterbury, who was executed by Queen Mary I as a heretic in 1556. Below far right, English philosopher Francis Bacon (1561–1626).

111

The rule of Britannia

The invasion of England in 1066 by the Normans, under the leadership of William the Conqueror, produced dramatic changes in the native Anglo-Saxon culture. Quick to adopt the Norman feudal system, the English created an aristocracy based on land tenure that was to dominate England for the next several centuries.

The struggle between English nobles for control of the Crown and the local government in the fifteenth century culminated in the dynastic conflict known as the Wars of the Roses. Richard, duke of York and leader of the Yorkist faction, defeated King Henry VI, of the rival House of Lancaster, at St. Albans in 1455—the first of a series of sporadic engagements that continued until 1485. In the latter year, at the battle of Bosworth Field, King Richard III, of the House of York was killed. The Lancastrian Henry Tudor founded a line that was to hold the throne for over two centuries.

Possessions of William the Conqueror

SCOTLAND
Edinburgh
York
IRELAND
KINGDOM OF
Dublin
ENGLAND
WALES
London
Exeter
Dover
Rouen
DUCHY OF
NORMANDY

**ENGLAND AND
THE NORMAN CONQUEST (1066)**

Territory subject to the Crown
★ Battles

KINGDOM OF
SCOTLAND
Edinburgh
Hexham (1464) ★
York
Lancaster ★ Towton
IRELAND
KINGDOM (1461)
Dublin
Bosworth Field (1485) ★ St. Albans
(1455,
Tewkesbury (1471) ★ 1461)
Barnet (1471) ★ London
OF ENGLAND

**THE WARS OF
THE ROSES (FIFTEENTH CENTURY)**

**GREAT BRITAIN
IN THE EIGHTEENTH CENTURY**

SCOTLAND
Edinburgh
Newcastle
IRELAND
Dublin
ENGLAND
WALES
London
Bristol
Southampton
Dover

Territory united with the Crown
under James I (1603) and by the
Act of Union of 1707

Territory united with the Crown
by the Act of Union of 1800

THE COLONIAL EXPANSION OF ENGLAND

NORTH AMERICA
Missouri
Mississippi
NEW FRANCE (1763)
Newfoundland (1713)
Acadia (1713)
Boston (1630)
Plymouth (1620)
Jamestown (1607)
ATLANTIC
Bermuda (1612)
Bahamas (1629)
Barbuda (1628)
Belize (1662)
Jamaica (1655)
Santa Lucia (1638)
Antigua (1632)
Fort James (1618)
Mosquito Coast (1687)
Barbados (1625)
Tasso (1663)
Sassandr (1664)
PACIFIC
OCEAN
Amazon
SOUTH AMERICA
Parana
St. Hel
OCEAN

Colonized in the sixteenth century
Colonized in the seventeenth century
Colonized in the eighteenth century
Colonized in the nineteenth century

Wales, an English principality since 1284, was incorporated with England in the first half of the sixteenth century, during the reign of one of the most famous Tudors, Henry VIII. Scotland, long at odds with its southern neighbor, was joined with England by the accession of King James VI of Scotland to the English throne as James I in 1603 and, formally, by the Act of Union of 1707. With the Act of Union of 1800, the United Kingdom of Great Britain and Ireland was formed and a single government created for the British Isles.

England began major overseas expansion in the seventeenth century, acquiring territory in North America and the Caribbean and trading posts in India and Africa. In the eighteenth century, after losing a sizable portion of its North American holdings as a result of the American Revolution (1775–1783), Britain set about building what is known as the Second British Empire. The entire continent of Australia, first settled by the British in 1788, was claimed in 1829. By 1887 those parts of India not under direct British control were governed by native rulers dependent on the British. The European partition of Africa in the late nineteenth century provided Britain with great expanses of territory in the southern half of the continent.

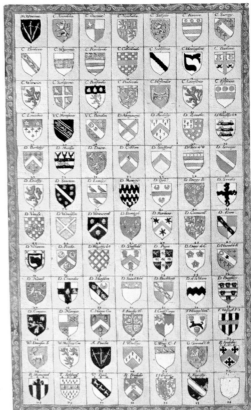

(begun by Edward I centuries earlier) and pressed against the Scots, whom he repeatedly defeated. Even so, the kingdom of Scotland refused to give way before him, forming its own alliance with France.

Henry VIII's early policy was determined by Wolsey, middle-class-man-made-good, who organized troops—and provisions and transport for them—in Henry's wars. As lord chancellor, archbishop of York, and then cardinal and papal legate (until his break with Henry in 1529), Wolsey ran the government. Arrogant and hungry for power, he advised Henry to align himself with France to achieve a balance of power—at that time a new diplomatic principle based

Queen Elizabeth opens a new session of Parliament (above left), and the Speaker of the House is presented (1584). The Tudor monarchs recognized the power Parliament had gained over issues of finance and were careful to accord it such respect as proved necessary. Top, a table of the counties constituting the realm of Elizabeth I. Immediately above, an English shilling bearing the profiles of Philip II of Spain and Mary I (Mary Tudor). Above right, a studio portrait of Elizabeth, by the noted Flemish painter Marcus Geerarts, the Younger.

on the formation of alliances to meet contingencies for the future. In the end, he fell from grace because he did not give Henry what the king wanted most: a divorce.

Henry, a knowledgeable supporter of Roman Catholic Orthodoxy, was named Defender of the Faith by the pope for his attack on Martin Luther. Ironically, Henry was the monarch who brought England to a permanent rupture with the papacy and the Church of Rome. The clash was based not so much on ecclesiastical reasons as on economic, political, and personal considerations. Fearing for the stability of his dynasty because his first wife, Catherine

of Aragon, had failed to produce a male heir, Henry decided upon a divorce. In an attempt to profit both politically and financially from the long-standing objection to papal interference in English affairs and to draw upon religion to support his belief in the absolute power of the monarchy, he used the pope's delay in granting his divorce as an excuse to sever the Catholic Church of England from Rome and to place himself at its head (grabbing massive Church spoils, or property, in the process). Although the English Church remained Catholic during Henry's reign, the monarch's refusal to be bound by traditional views opened the way to Calvinism and other nonconformist religions that contributed to the forthcoming Protestant Reformation.

Upon Henry's death in 1547, his ten-year-old son, Edward VI (produced by the third of Henry's six wives), ascended the throne. A Council of Regency ruled until Edward's death at sixteen, at which time Henry's daughter Mary, a religious reactionary, succeeded him as Mary I, or Mary Tudor.

Although Mary sought to undo the Reformation, she failed, lacking that most necessary of Renaissance qualities—politesse. When she went so far as to marry Philip II, a Spanish cousin who saw himself as defender of Catholicism—and later threw England into Spain's war against France, losing Calais, the last English outpost in Europe—the country rebelled. Except in Ireland, her subjects came to hate her. Ordering those she viewed as heretics burned at the stake (earning the name Bloody Mary), she created Protestant martyrs throughout the land, and her power faltered. As one martyr, Hugh Latimer, said in comforting another as they were led to the stake, "Be of good comfort, we shall this day light such a candle, by God's grace, in England, as I trust shall never be put out." Mary's death in 1558 ended all hope for Catholicism in England.

Elizabeth was the third of Henry's children to wear the crown. The Virgin Queen—her name immortalized in the name Virginia, the first colony in the New World, the true beginnings of empire—both reigned and ruled. Alternating tolerance and repression, she concentrated her enormous abilities on developing control over the seas, founding new colonies, and promoting trade: She was centrally responsible for the spacious times of which the Victorian poet Alfred Lord Tennyson would write three hundred and fifty years later as he intentionally linked in the public mind England's two grandest reigns, those of Elizabeth and of the contemporary queen, Victoria.

Elizabeth was the symbol of England triumphant; the buccaneer Francis Drake, who in 1577 led the first English expedition to circumnavigate the globe, for which he was knighted in 1580, was the symbol of a British Empire emergent. The moment that assured British supremacy came in the summer of 1588 and was based, in part, on the circumstances surrounding Mary Stuart, the Catholic Queen of Scotland. Married to the heir to the throne of France (having spent most of her early years in that country), Mary claimed the English throne on the grounds that Elizabeth was illegitimate, and a reluctant Elizabeth had in turn supported a Protestant rebellion in Scotland aimed at forcing Mary to oust her French Catholic allies. After Mary bore the future James VI of Scotland, she married a Protestant lover, the earl of Both-

verde onthalst Maria

Mary Stuart, Queen of Scots, is one of the most romantic heroines of history because of her tragic life. Ultimately deprived of two queenships many believe were rightfully hers, implicated in the murder of her lover Lord Darnley, and charged with plotting to murder Queen Elizabeth, Mary maneuvered skillfully to retain her kingdom and to maintain Catholicism in Scotland. In the end, however, she failed and was executed at Fotheringhay castle (left) while clutching her crucifix.

Left, the palace and abbey of Holyrood in Edinburgh. Begun by James IV in 1501, it was the favorite residence of generations of Scottish kings. When Oliver Cromwell's anti-royalist forces occupied the building in 1650, much was destroyed. The present Holyrood house is now the official residence in Scotland of Britain's reigning monarch.

When Mary Stuart (right) stepped down from the Scottish throne in 1567, her son succeeded her as James VI of Scotland; her brother James Stuart became regent on behalf of the infant king and was assassinated under mysterious circumstances in 1570. Below, a posthumous picture showing his wounds.

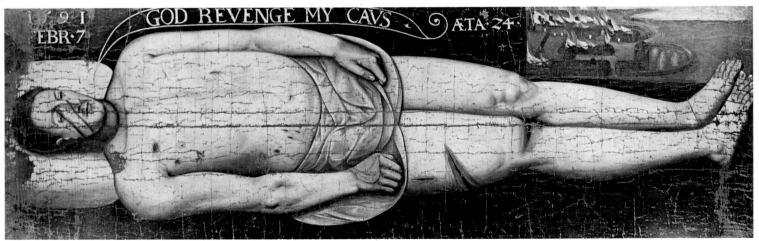

Right, a frequently encountered portrait of Shakespeare. Above, William Hogarth's rendering of a scene from The Tempest. *In the eighteenth century Shakespeare's works were purged of their "vulgarity" and were given, as in this painting, "classical" or "idealized" form, obviously distorting the intent of the artist.*

Center left, a model of the second Globe Theatre. Such models became standard equipment in drama schools as Shakespeare came to dominate staging as well as the play. Left and below, two views of Shakespeare's birthplace (now a museum) at Stratford-on-Avon, where the poet was born to his globemaker father and prosperous landed mother in 1564.

Shakespeare, the theatrical genius

William Shakespeare dominated the literary scene as Elizabeth I did the political, and as historian and poet, he reveled in the rough history of British royalty. No author in all literature is so often quoted. "Uneasy lies the head that wears a crown," he wrote, and proved it so in play after play about the monarchs of England. Some might think him cynical, but his audiences knew him to be a patriot, and they filled the Globe and later the Blackfriars Theatre to hear his words about "this blessed plot, this earth, this realm, this England." And yet, we know perplexingly little about him: Even his name was spelled in many ways, and some claim that his finest plays and most beautiful sonnets were the work of others. Not since the ancient Greeks had theatre so flourished in the Western world, and for this achievement Shakespeare was primarily responsible.

Every significant English playwright before Shakespeare was a university man; he was the first to rise from the often despised community of actors. Born in 1564, he married Anne Hathaway in 1582, and they had three children. Shakespeare died in 1616, after having written some 37 plays and 154 sonnets.

Left, the home of Mary Arden, Shakespeare's mother, at Wilmcote. The playwright's own house has not survived, having been torn down in 1759. The British rediscovered their pride in Shakespeare in 1847; when it appeared that his birthplace as well would be destroyed, the Shakespeare Birthplace Trust, which has since preserved many properties, was formed. The Wilmcote house itself was rescued in 1930.

Left, Holy Trinity, parish church of Stratford, where Shakespeare is buried beneath a tombstone that reads, "Good friend for Jesus sake forbeare, to digg the dust encloased heare. Blese be ye man y spares thes stones and curst be he ty move my bones"—this to prevent the bones from being thrown into the charnel house, the customary receptacle. Right, a watercolor of the Globe Theatre by Wenceslaus Hollar. Demolished by the Puritans, the theatre was viewed as the work of the devil.

well, who was widely believed to have murdered his chief rival for her hand; she thus sealed her fate, for she lost her support among even the Catholics. Forced to abdicate in favor of her infant son, she sought refuge in England, where Elizabeth had her imprisoned in a guarded castle. When it became known that even then Mary plotted against the Crown, Parliament asked Elizabeth to order Mary's execution, which she did in 1587 (with every appearance of reluctance).

King Philip II of Spain—like his father, Holy Roman Emperor Charles V, a great defender of Catholicism—witnessed the defeat of the Catholic forces internally in England and Scotland and decided that only by war might he win England back to Catholicism. Also realizing that the Elizabethan seadogs, with their piratings and lootings, would soon harry the Spanish from the seas (especially in the Caribbean) if not soundly defeated, Philip sent 131 ships in one great armada against England in 1588. Drake, one of Elizabeth's most spirited commanders, immediately launched a surprise attack against the Spanish fleet while still at anchor. Against the Spanish Armada, the English then hurled 197 smaller ships of greater maneuverability, manned by better gunners and sailors than those of Spain, and largely supplied

by private enterprise. The Spanish were vanquished, with only seventy-six ships returning home. On just this kind of daring, flexibility, and private commitment would the British Empire grow.

Although England did not win any significant Spanish territory in its many conflicts with Spain during Elizabeth's reign, the defeat of the Spanish Armada may be seen as a great psychological victory for the English as well as a victory for the survival of Protestantism both in England and in Scotland (for political as well as moral reasons, Ireland would remain Catholic). Thus would this great war with Spain—to be followed by the first great war for em-

Top, a painting by Philip II's official portraitist, Juan Pantoja de la Cruz, of the conference held in 1604 at London's Somerset House to establish peace between England and Spain. Immediately above, the Armada portrait of Elizabeth I, perhaps the finest example of Elizabethan court art. She is shown as an ageless beauty, though nearing sixty. Right, a painting depicting the clash between the English and Spanish fleets in 1588.

Details of two paintings on canvas by the Dutch artist Adam Willaerts show less dramatic aspects of maritime life (above left). Left, a depiction of doctors administering to a patient. The room is hung in scarlet to indicate that the patient is the victim of a fever. Doctors tended to focus on the symptom of the disease—the fever—rather than the disease itself, and purging "bad blood" was a common treatment. Religion, science, and magic are intertwined, though unconsciously, in the painting.

The Chariott drawne by foure Horses vpon which charret stood the Coffin couered wth purple Veluett and vpon that the representation, The Canapy borne by six Knights.

pire, with Catholic France—shape the emerging *British* nation domestically.

Yet it was not only the battle with the Spanish Armada that instilled in the English a feeling of confidence and triumph in their conflicts with Spain. It was, perhaps most of all, Elizabeth, the Imperial Virgin, who did so. Around her would form a cult of chivalry; from her would grow a variety of symbolism that, drawing most clearly on the image of Elizabeth as Astraea, goddess of justice, combined classical and Christian views; by her would be promoted a conscious imitation of the dazzling splendor of Holy Roman Emperor and Spanish king Charles V, who, as the inheritor of Philip I, sought to give Spain and the Hapsburgs a universal empire. Elizabeth knew that the empire was based on an act of theatre and

Elizabeth had sought to ward off loneliness by drawing favorites to her side, but she died on March 24, 1603, of "a heavy dullness, with a frowardness familiar to old age." On April 28, the date of her funeral, a life-size effigy under a black canopy was drawn through the streets by knights accompanied by gentlemen pensioners (above).

Henry VIII's life had, in part, been determined by women; Elizabeth's was much influenced by men. Facing page, below, left to right: Robert Dudley, earl of Leicester, who hoped to marry the queen; Sir Thomas Gresham, who created the Royal Exchange; Sir Nicholas Bacon, lord keeper of the great (royal) seal; and Sir John Dodderidge, chief justice to the queen.

This page, below, left to right: explorer Sir Walter Raleigh, who named Virginia after the Virgin Queen Elizabeth; the earl of Essex, who ousted Raleigh from the favor of the queen; Sir Henry Sidney, lord deputy of Ireland; and Sir Francis Drake, who commanded the first English voyage around the world.

James I (below) did not want war with Spain, but Parliament and his advisers did; they forced a naval war upon the king in 1624. Above, a British attack on the Spanish in the Caribbean, 1624. Left, Castle Stalker, built by the Stewart clan of Scotland against the English.

that it also depended on loyalty: She had an unerring eye on how to command both. When Elizabeth died in 1603 without heirs, Mary Stuart's son, James VI, king of Scotland, ascended the English throne as James I. He thus created the kingdom of Great Britain—formally united a century later—consisting of England, Scotland, and Wales (which had been incorporated with England in the sixteenth century), and inherited as his right a strong and united nation.

Indeed, perhaps too strong and united, for as the nation came to sense that a strong monarchy no longer was the mainstay of the people's welfare, the popularity of the Crown waned. James I, who believed in the divine right of kings, contributed through bad management, a poor choice of advisers, and plain bullheadedness to that decline. The nation had not fought a war against popery to succumb to authoritarianism in the form of monarchy. James was suspected of having designs on Parliament and although Protestant, he was clearly anti-Puritan, for he knew that this religious group (consisting of English Calvinists who wanted all traces of Catholicism expunged from the Church of England) was aligned against monarchy—and all rank. He and his successor, his son Charles I, also authoritarian, came into conflict with Parliament over their desire for in-

To avoid war with Spain, James sent his son Charles to woo and marry the infanta Maria of Spain. Negotiations went badly, and Prince Charles returned to Plymouth with his fleet (below) in 1623. Englishmen rejoiced, for they had feared a Spanish match would destroy Protestantism in England.

When Parliament protested the taxes needed to support war with Spain, Charles I (right) dissolved it, only to have to recall Parliament and accept restrictions on his power. His authoritarian policies and religious intolerance led Scotland to rise in rebellion in 1638.

creased taxation. Condemning Charles for High Church Anglicanism—that is, for being soft on Catholicism—Parliament sought to block his every move, and the king accordingly refused to call Parliament into session.

In this climate of religious tension and apprehension, thousands were leaving Britain in search of religious freedom as they defined it, first for Holland and then for the New World. They were harbingers of an empire for a new reason. Three types of colonies would evolve in North America in which religious minorities could seek refuge: those chartered and governed by companies, as in Massachusetts; those directly under the Crown, as in Virginia; and those under proprietors owing their allegiance to the Crown, such as Maryland. Religious tensions in Britain, however, were transported, in translated form, to the colonies, where American Calvinists renewed the war against Catholicism in the New World.

James had left to his son a legacy of problems. He had begun the colonization of northern Ireland with Protestants, which led to revolt there. By the time Charles came to power, Puritans bent on toppling the Crown had taken control of Parliament, and a public proclamation summarized Puritan grievances against Charles. Civil war followed in 1642, as the Anglicans—who disliked the Puritans on religious grounds, wishing to retain a religious hierarchy—coalesced into Royalists. While the gentry generally supported the king, a minority led by Oliver Cromwell did not, supporting the parliamentarians, who drew their strength from the townspeople demographically and from the Puritans religiously.

Organizing a New Model Army, Cromwell drove the Royalists from the field. Soon England was governed by a military despotism which, to survive, had to execute the king: Charles Stuart was beheaded in 1649. By dying with dignity, he discredited the kangaroo court that had tried him, and ironically the people came to see the king as the defender of their liberties against arbitrary judgment. His martyrdom saved the monarchy as an institution, for the anarchy that accompanied the following interregnum, known as the Commonwealth or the Protectorate (1649–1660), convinced even a freely elected Parliament that it must, for stability, restore the monarchy.

Still, Oliver Cromwell had worked to make England great, for it was under him that the Navigation Acts were codified. The Navigation Act of 1651 required that goods brought to English ports arrive in English vessels or in those of the countries of origin, eliminating the middleman (who was usually Dutch or French). This attempt to strangle Dutch trade led to a war in which the Dutch were vanquished, and peace was made in 1654. England now entered its most productive period of international trade prior to the nineteenth century.

Trade was strengthened by the principle of enumerated goods, items that the colonists could carry only to English ports, or in their own coastal trade, so

In 1653 Oliver Cromwell dissolved the thirteen-year-old Long Parliament (left), assumed the title Lord Protector, and instituted a new form of government that became increasingly repressive. After Charles I's execution under Cromwell in 1649, and the Scot's subsequent recognition of Charles II as king, Cromwell invaded (and later annexed) Scotland, defeating a veteran army twice the size of his own at Dunbar in 1650 (below left). Below, Cromwell's soldiers during the early phase of the Civil War (1642–1646), or the Great Revolution, which ended in the temporary abolition of the monarchy.

that they could not develop links with potential enemies of England, as in the French West Indies; by the capture of Jamaica from the Spanish in 1655; and by the growth of the British East India Company, the great private trading company established during Elizabeth's reign which eventually became, in India, a tremendously wealthy and powerful governing body as well. Milton, whose *Paradise Lost* demonstrated the continued significance of religion to the British, might have been speaking for the secular side of the British nation as well when he wrote: "The world was all before them, where to choose/Their place of rest, and Providence their guide."

Charles I's son Charles II, in refuge in France, was invited to return to inaugurate the Restoration, or the re-establishment of the monarchy, in 1660. Some-

what of a skeptic, interested in science and a noncontentious life, Charles was prepared to reign while Parliament ruled. The people, who were aware with poet John Milton that the "New Presbyters" (the followers of Cromwell during the Commonwealth) had, in the end, proved to be "but old priest[s] writ large," supported the restoration of the Church of England and welcomed the resurgence of theatre, art, and music that had been suppressed by the Puritan regime, and that now followed Charles II's return.

When James II succeeded his brother Charles II in 1685, he sought to restore Catholicism, but it was much too late, for by now Parliament spoke of itself with a capital *P*. Parliament accepted James II only on the condition that on his death, succession would go to his eldest daughter, Mary, wife of William of Orange, who was the Protestant leader of the young,

Oliver Cromwell's reputation is a study in changing fashion. Those who respect power respect him. In America, Theodore Roosevelt would write an admiring biography; in France, his portrait would hang at Versailles. Called by some a philistine, Cromwell (left) was an uncompromising and able statesman and politician. Edmund Burke, formulator of the self-conscious political conservatism of the late eighteenth century, wrote of him, "Cromwell was a man in whom ambition had not wholly suppressed, but only suspended, the sentiments of religion." Above, Cromwell's death mask, molded at the leader's funeral.

Charles II (above left) was recalled from exile and restored to the throne in 1660. Top, George Monck, who arranged for Charles' return. Immediately above, Richard Rainsford, commissioner for the rebuilding of London after the Great Fire of 1666, from Gerald Soest's official portrait, ca. 1678.

independent, now anti-Catholic and anti-Spanish Dutch Republic. When the king's third son was baptized a Catholic in 1688, Parliament sought to remove James II from the throne: William of Orange peacefully landed troops in England on the invitation of leaders from the newly emerging political parties—the Whigs and Tories—and claimed the throne, to rule jointly with Mary. This, the Glorious (or Bloodless) Revolution of 1688, assured a continued monarchy, an ascendant Parliament, prosperity for Scotland, political liberty for England—and war, political oppression, and economic depression for Catholic Ireland. It also assured war with France, as William of Orange had been the leader of the European opposition to the French king Louis XIV.

So began the great march to an empire that would embrace the continents. William understood, as did his successors, that the war for Europe now had to be a world war, for the English navy would be pitted against the great power of the French, who had forces stationed all over the world: A victory on the Conti-

nent, as at Blenheim, Bavaria, during the War of the Spanish Succession in 1704, might be rendered null by a defeat overseas. Now began the "swarming" of the English—exploration and discovery in North America, the Pacific, and Asia; the opening of settler colonies along the length of North America; the use of blacks from Africa as slaves to assure a dependable labor supply in growing sugar, tobacco, and cotton, as the colonies in America and the Caribbean in turn became a market garden to Britain's empire. War with France would be almost continuous, lasting until the final vanquishment of France from North America as a result of the British victory on the icy

The enormous palace of Hampton Court (courtyard, left) was begun in 1514 by Cardinal Thomas Wolsey, then passed on to Henry VIII; in the seventeenth century, the residence was modified by the great architect Christopher Wren. In 1670 Charles II joined France's Louis XIV in an unpopular war on the United Provinces of the Netherlands. Above, the English Royal James *under attack by Dutch fire ships at the battle of Southwold Bay, 1672.*

Plains of Abraham, above Quebec, in 1759.

In time would come a vast movement of south Asians, of Indians who would be displaced into the West Indies, East Africa, and the Pacific Islands as laborers (and, eventually, mercenary soldiers and small merchants) for the empire. The ethnographic map of the world would be remade, and that remaking would transform Britain itself. By the time Queen Anne replaced her elder sister Mary in 1702, the tenets of mercantile theory—establishing a circle of commerce by which a favorable balance of trade was attained—were commonplace. Britain was Queen of the Seas.

In 1704 the British took Gibraltar, off southern Spain, and thus assured their dominance of the mouth of the Mediterranean. At mid-century, in 1757, Robert Clive defeated a vast Indian army at Plassey in West Bengal, assuring British ascendancy over the French and leading several years later to the founding of the empire of British India. In 1763 French Canada passed into British hands at the end of the Seven Years' War. True, by 1783 Britain had lost a major portion of its North American empire, but it had begun an empire—the Second British Empire, as it is now called by historians—equally as great in south and Southeast Asia, in Australia, and early in the next century, in southern Africa.

In 1701, Parliament asserted its power—never again successfully denied—to primacy. By the Act of Succession that year it determined that the throne would pass not through the Stuarts (who were Catholic) but through the Protestant German House of Hanover. George I, elector of Hanover, who derived

his descent through James I, became king in 1714; since he did not speak English, he did not attend cabinet meetings, further assuring the growth of Parliament, and especially of cabinet government, and even more specifically of the Whigs who after 1721 were led for twenty-one years by Sir Robert Walpole. Coarse, reserved, slow, George was an intensely unpopular ruler.

Under George II, who reigned from 1727 to 1760, the cabinet became the true center of power. While Parliament was, in fact, a series of cliques and factions, the machinery for the democratic system that would become the model for constitutions the world over was in the making. In time it would be Parliament, not the Crown, that would force reform upon the British East India Company, which had taken over enormous territories, ruling like a sovereign power.

Increasingly, life in Georgian England was becoming town-centered, and it was the gentry, the country squire, who was setting the cultural tone. Already

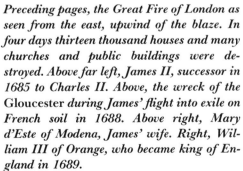

Preceding pages, the Great Fire of London as seen from the east, upwind of the blaze. In four days thirteen thousand houses and many churches and public buildings were destroyed. Above far left, James II, successor in 1685 to Charles II. Above, the wreck of the Gloucester during James' flight into exile on French soil in 1688. Above right, Mary d'Este of Modena, James' wife. Right, William III of Orange, who became king of England in 1689.

England was growing crowded—indeed, by 1600 the population density of England had reached that of the United States in 1961—and was giving thought to sending people to the colonies for yet other reasons: opportunities for less expensive land and, generally, a better life. But above all the colonies were tempting to those who sought a more open political atmosphere—as did the Thetford corsetmaker Thomas Paine when he set out for America in 1774, where he wrote his famous pamphlet, *Common Sense.* Theatre,

English society in the eighteenth century

England possessed the eighteenth century, some historians say, for it was a time of extraordinary growth—overseas as well as at home—in power and prestige, in the arts, and in political thought. It was also a century of exceptional elegance in manners and dress—and of exceptional squalor for the poor. Social advantage was centered on ownership of land, and the traditional aristocracy remained strong; at the same time, the "counter-jumping class"—merchants who formed the core of the rising middle class and came to be important in the development of the empire—were growing in number and influence. No artist more perfectly captured the paradox of the age—elegance in the midst of degradation—than William Hogarth, satirist and master painter of the "high life of society." His success began in 1732 with the first of his series of "moral pictures," *The Harlot's Progress*, an allegory of the times.

Far left, from Hogarth's Morning after the Wedding, *part of his* Marriage à la Mode, *an attack on the fashionable marriage of convenience. The poet (near left) reads to Lord George Graham, a "poetaster," or aristocratic patron. Below, far left, a violinist from* A Musical Evening, *one of a series in* The Rake's Progress. *Below left, Hogarth's great canvas from* The Rake's Progress, *satirizing popular vices.*

Top right, Hogarth's The Gates of Calais. *Immediately above, a detail depicting Bedlam, the infamous lunatic asylum. Right, the arrest of a debtor. Below,* The Poet in Misery *being presented with bills.*

the coffee house, the rise of political debating and oratory of a higher order, the slow infusion of Enlightenment thought, all elevated the intellectual life of the nation. Unhappily for the first Hanoverian king who wanted to rule as well as reign, the doctrines of the Enlightenment philosophers of France and of their early English confrere, John Locke, took at least as deep root in the American colonies. Great Britain, which had become the first modern state, would now face in America the first modern war—a revolution fought by guerrilla tactics.

Had the British not so thoroughly defeated the French in North America, perhaps there would have been no revolution. But in removing the Gallic peril that bound the colonies to their loyalty to Britain, the British army had given impetus to the freer spirit in America. Yet a Parliament that had newly, and hardly, won its own prerogatives, was not inclined to pass them easily to a colonial people who, the British felt, drew more benefits from, than they gave to, the empire.

symbol more than the fact of taxation was made evident when they protested this tax as well, dumping the East India Company's tea in Boston harbor and switching to coffee. Britain retaliated by closing Boston's port. In 1774 a Congress drawn from the colonies convened in Philadelphia; the next year open warfare broke out.

The American Revolution was a civil war within the British nation. Although the colonists did not initially intend independence, even as they fought, the war both energized them and heightened their sense of grievance. Once realizing that foreign assistance was needed, they also concluded that the French were unlikely to intervene unless the colonists declared their intent to fight to the end. United as never before in the furnace of warfare, the Americans declared themselves to be independent on July 4, 1776. They have, ever since, celebrated their independence on the anniversary of that date—the only people in the world who still declare themselves to be a nation simply because they asserted it to be so at a precise moment

At the outset, the Americans did not want to be independent; they wanted a voice in their taxation and they wanted to reassert their rights as Englishmen, rights they felt King George III was infringing. Increasingly the "American question" dominated British party politics. When the British imposed a duty on the colonies for the first time in 1763, they did not realize they had set upon the long path to open warfare. In 1770 the British repealed all duties save that on tea; that the colonists objected to the

The English gained one of their greatest victories at the Bavarian town of Blenheim, on August 13, 1704. There, John Churchill, first duke of Marlborough, and Prince Eugene of Savoy commanded a combined Anglo-Austrian force against the French (Flemish tapestry, above). Above right, the Thames at Horseferry, with Lambeth Palace—the residence of the archbishop of Canterbury—on the right and old houses of Parliament on the left. Right, Queen Anne, the last Stuart monarch, succeeding William and Mary in 1702.

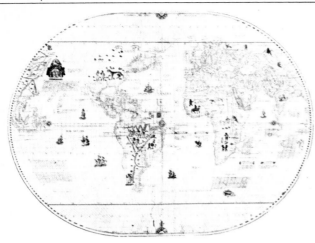

Left, Sebastian Cabot's map of the world, printed in 1544, while he was seeking a northeast passage to Asia. Below, Captain James Cook's two exploring vessels, the Resolution and the Adventure, off Tahiti, as painted by William Hodges. Bottom left, Admiral Horatio Nelson, British victor at Trafalgar, where in 1805 the British defeated the combined French and Spanish fleets; center, Captain Cook in 1776; right, Sir Edward Hawke, victor at Quiberon Bay, Canada, in 1759.

Above, French ships attacking the British at Quebec in 1759. Defeated at Quiberon and Quebec, the French lost all hope of invading Britain. Facing page, top, Portsmouth, England, in the eighteenth century. Right, some of the cannons on Nelson's flag ship Victory.

The British navy, ruler of the seas

Though an island people, the British were slow to reap the harvest of the sea or to use the water as a bridge to other lands. Attacks and incursions from foreign invaders, however, at last alerted the British to the need to control their own waters. In the ninth century each county supplied the sovereign with ships for the common defense against the Norse Vikings. By the end of the seventeenth century, the English supplanted the Dutch and the Spanish navies. By the eighteenth century only the French navy could match the British, and after the naval reforms of 1832, the Royal Navy became the most powerful in the world, truly ruling the waves. It was unexcelled by any other nation until the 1920s and unsurpassed until World War Two.

Several factors contributed to British maritime superiority. They mastered the haven-finding art (that is, navigation), borrowing and buying talent from other nations; this strategy helped to place them at the forefront of the systematic exploration of the eighteenth century, by which they would claim many additional lands for their empire as well as naval bases and fueling stations. Their naval architecture also improved as decks, hulls, and rigging were adjusted to produce lighter, faster ships that could maneuver more easily in battle. British technology eventually outstripped all others, leading to the abandonment of the one-cannon galley (favored by the French) for multigun frigates capable of firing great distances with great flexibility, and then for carronades (close-range cannons), lethal against human targets.

Between 1746 and 1753 the great Italian painter Canaletto worked in England, creating some of the most finely detailed scenes of stately life in existence. Above, his detail of the New Horse Guards, or barracks, still under construction in 1753. Below, Westminster Abbey behind a procession of the Knights of the Order of the Bath, 1749. Below right, a Canaletto canvas showing the Rotunda at Ranelagh, painted after his return to Italy in 1754, probably from memory. Ranelagh was a pleasure garden near London opened in 1742; the Rotunda, which appears in all social annals of the day, was a hallmark of "the fashionable life."

in time. The British thought otherwise, but brilliant tactics by the Americans, led by General George Washington, and the intervention of the French, especially on the seas, brought world war, Lord Cornwallis' defeat at Yorktown in 1781, and American freedom at last through negotiations at Versailles in 1783.

Two weeks after Yorktown, but before the news of defeat had reached England, George III wrote to his prime minister, Lord North, "The die is now cast whether this [Britain] shall be a great empire or the least dignified of European States." The king knew that Britain, dwarfed in Europe by France and overseas even yet by Spain, would be plunged into a debilitating struggle for survival. In 1783 the defeated king therefore dismissed the cabinet and placed the ministry in the hands of William Pitt, the Younger (son of the great statesman William Pitt, the Elder), to build a new empire.

The Second British Empire was based less on settlement—as in North America—and more on the exploitation of primarily nonwhite lands. It was also based on the Industrial Revolution, which in turn it fed. Britain would become not just the first modern state but, in the nineteenth century, the first modernized nation, for it would experience first all the benefits and the ills of industrialization. A profound upheaval followed upon the great British textile industry inventions—the flying shuttle, the spinning jenny, the power loom—and later new developments in the iron industry. The last stimulated the coal industry. The steam engine, initially applied in cotton spinning, then to mining and metallurgical industries, increased output tenfold. The tyranny of the factory bell stimulated working men to organize themselves, as the demand for labor soared, due to the new machinery which so reduced prices for manufactured goods that demand for goods outgrew supply. The colonies provided outlets for these manufactured goods as well as sources of raw material.

This new British Empire was based upon another event that occurred in 1776, one at least as important as the North American revolution: the publication of Adam Smith's *Wealth of Nations*. Smith effectively opposed the old system of mercantilism, which controlled trade. The younger Pitt was convinced of Smith's argument: that free trade and competition would best promote the national welfare. Production was more important than commerce; if each individual could follow his own interests, consumable goods (the best form of wealth) would increase, production and trade would flow into profitable channels, and competition would assure that prices remained rea-

sonable, completing a quite different circle of commerce, one based on independence and increased national productivity.

This argument, that of *laissez faire*, or "let alone," became the basis for the new imperialism of free trade. Britain, knowing itself to be in the lead in the industrial race—being able to produce the most goods at the cheapest price, and transport them at the greatest speed—naturally advocated lowering tariff barriers between nations and their empires. Only during the latter part of the nineteenth century did some British turn away from free trade imperialism to advocate once again, as they had before the American

Left, George II, the last English king to lead his troops in combat, at the battle of Dettingen in 1743. Above, Sir Robert Walpole. Below, the battle of Culloden.

Revolution, a variety of forms of protectionism (which they often disguised under the phrase "fair trade").

Meanwhile the great war with France for mastery of the world continued. In 1789 the French nation had been shaken to its roots by a revolution of its own, far bloodier than the American, brought on by rising prices that resulted, in part, from the aid to the Americans. In 1793 France declared war on Britain, and at Toulon the British were blown away by artillery under a twenty-four-year-old officer, Napoleon Bonaparte. Napoleon would oppose Britain from that day until the battle of Waterloo, in 1815, and the former American colonies would be drawn into the War of 1812, into renewed conflict with the once honored Mother Country.

The jewel of the new empire was India, which in 1858 would come directly under British control, the power of the East India Company having been abolished following the Indian Mutiny of 1857–1859. At home the Crown grew ever weaker as Parliament asserted its strength, and in 1832, through the Great Reform Bill, extended the right to vote in the first of three great democratizing steps. (Other reform bills would follow in 1867 and 1918.) Railway building reached out across the British Isles and throughout

A View of the Taking of QUEBEC September 1.ᵗʰ 1759   *Vue de la Prise de QUEBEC le 13 Septembre 1759.*

Right, the Young Pretender, Charles Edward Stuart, or Bonnie Prince Charlie. Son of the Old Pretender, James Edward, and grandson of James II, he had hoped to claim the British throne. After a victory at Prestonpans in Scotland in 1745, Charles Edward set out to invade England, but his Catholic cause was crushed in April of 1746 at Culloden, in the Scottish Highlands. Charles Edward's French allies were virtually vanquished from their vast North American empire thirteen years later, when the English, arriving via the St. Lawrence River, ascended to the Plains of Abraham above Quebec (above) and compelled the French to surrender. During the battle both commanders, the French Montcalm and the English Wolfe, lost their lives.

143

Left, a portrait of King George III in his coronation robes, by Allan Ramsay (1760). Above, George III at a military parade in Hyde Park in 1799, the year in which Napoleon had seized power in France as first consul.

Right, a contemporary print of Havana being occupied by British troops in 1762, during the Seven Years' War. The next year Havana was returned to Spain, for which the British people blamed George III.

Above, William Pitt, the Younger (1759–1806), as painted by Thomas Gainsborough. William Pitt, the Elder (1708–1778), greatest orator of his time, had opposed the harsh policy forced upon the American colonists by "the king's friends" but had retired in 1768, ill; his second son became prime minister in 1783 and led Britain in its Continental war against France. Left, a detail of Covent Garden Market.

the empire—especially in India—and the railway passenger coach made cheap seaside holidays available to the British for the first time. Both a new sense of leisure and a new urgency of work overtook the nation, and the characteristically British virtues of duty, thrift, courtesy, and integrity asserted themselves as never before.

These characteristics of the British are often said to be Victorian, for they were much in evidence during the reign of that incredible monarch. A somewhat dumpy woman who stood four feet, ten inches tall (and four feet, two inches wide), she gave the nation in all its classes a sense of pride, a persistent belief that God was an Englishman (or, at the very least, spoke English). During Victoria's reign from 1837 to 1901 the face of England changed. Health, personal relations, and individual creativity were sacrificed to the demands of production; cities sprang up in the place of green fields; the population of Britain exploded, increasing fifty percent in forty years. Rookeries, or great slums, increased fourfold.

The joint exploitation of coal and iron transformed both the system of production and social life. Once the coal-fed furnaces were accepted as the most efficient and profitable method of smelting iron, increased effort was needed for the extraction of these

two minerals, and coal mines in particular required more and more labor. The mine owners did not hesitate to force even women and children to work fourteen hours a day in the pits, seldom to see the sun, some of whom scarcely benefited from the well-intentioned but ill-enforced reform legislation that was eventually passed. It was not only rivers and hills that were polluted with mine slag: It was lives as well. Nor was it only the hills that were denuded for charcoal, then marred by pit faces, as one scarce energy supply was supplanted by another: So too was the human spirit.

Yet, Britain had been more successful at ridding itself of another evil—slavery. A body of humanitarians known as the Saints had attacked the overseas slave trade, for they knew that if they could limit the operations of those who traded in human beings, the price of slaves would soar, and slave owners would move more quickly to machine labor, especially in the new United States. After achieving this first goal in 1807, the abolitionists struck against the institution of slavery itself, and in 1833 slavery was abolished throughout the British Empire. This helped place an even greater strain on its retention in the United States and elsewhere assured that, as arguments for white supremacy developed at the Cape of Good

While on a mission to London, an officer in Napoleon's army, Vincenzo Lunardi, inaugurated the air age by ascending in a hydrogen-filled balloon from Moorfields (above) in September of 1784. Below, The Iron Forge *(1772), by Joseph Wright of Derby, one of the first leading English artists to depict scientific and industrial interests.*

As England became industrialized, steam replaced hydraulic power and coke replaced charcoal in furnaces. Today ruined engine-houses dot Cornwall, especially on Bolenowe Moors. Near right, a steam whim at Pool, used to haul ore to the surface. Far right, plans for constructing a hydraulic engine (1794). Below right, a schematic drawing showing a cross-section of an eighteenth-century English mine.

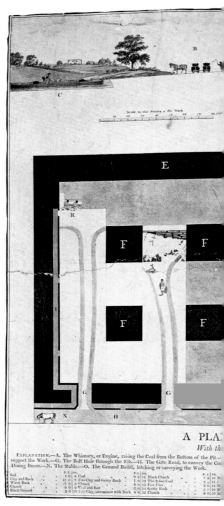

A PLA

With th

EXPLANATION.—A. The Whimsey, or Engine, raising the Coal from the Bottom of the Pit.
support the Work.—G. The Bolt Hole through the Rib.—H. The Gate Road, to convey the Coa
Dining Room.—N. The Stable.—O. The Ground Bailiff, latching or surveying the Work.

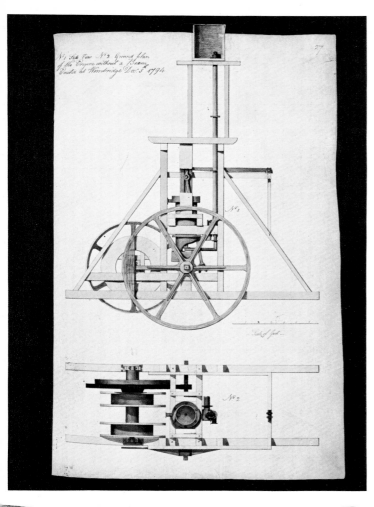

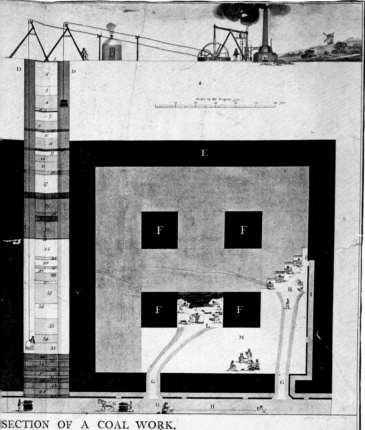

SECTION OF A COAL WORK,
y met with in sinking, near Wednesbury, Staffordshire.

Hope, slavery was not one of the options open to colonial legislators there.

The way was cleared for a free trading British Empire to reach out to the world. In 1839 the Durham Report, advocating self-government for Canada, initiated the move to responsible government; in 1867 the British North American colonies would enter into the Canadian Confederation, becoming the first self-governing colony within the empire. As Lord Durham wrote his report, the British occupied Aden (the vital fueling station on the southern tip of the Arabian Peninsula) to guard the southern entrance to the Red Sea. Once his report was published, the British entered into the first Afghan War and, shortly thereafter, the first Chinese War which yielded, in 1842, the colony of Hong Kong. In 1840 Britain annexed New Zealand, assuring the Maori tribesmen protection, by Queen Victoria, of their rights as British subjects and of possession of their land: Within a few years Her Majesty's Maori subjects were at war with Her Majesty's imperial troops. In India, Sind in 1843, the Punjab in 1849, and Oudh in 1856 were annexed. Lagos, on the Nigerian coast, was added in 1861. The click of dates, like the click of railway wheels, as imperial engineers and native labor moved the empire forward at the average rate of thirty-three rails per hour, marked almost irresistible growth: the Gold Coast of Africa in 1871, the first three Malay states in 1874, the Fiji Islands the same year, Cyprus in 1878 under the Treaty of Berlin, Borneo in 1881, New Guinea in 1884, Burma in 1886. From coastal enclaves the British pressed toward the interior of both the Asian and African continents.

Perhaps above all, two developments marked the spirit of British imperialism in the second half of the nineteenth century. The first was the opening of the Suez Canal in 1869, which cut the voyage to India—heretofore around the Cape of Good Hope—from four months to less than a month. Now India and the Orient were moved far closer together with this joining of the Mediterranean and Red seas. In 1875 the nearly bankrupt ruler of Egypt, Khedive Ismail, sold his shares in the canal to the British government, with the English prime minister Benjamin Disraeli organizing a secret loan. Control of the canal was now in British hands.

The second event captured the imagination of the imperial British as no other event did: the reconquest of the Sudan in Africa. There, in 1885, the Mahdist Sudanese (followers of the Mahdi, a Moslem religious leader) had stormed the city of Khartoum and killed "Chinese" Gordon—British hero of the empire—and his men. Twelve years later, on the eve of the sixtieth anniversary of Queen Victoria's reign, Sir Herbert

Above, an Anglo-Spanish fleet carrying refugees from Toulon, in southern France, where an unsuccessful rebellion against the revolutionary government in Paris occurred in 1793. Below, a coin struck for George III in 1817. Right, the duke of Wellington, as portrayed by Sir Thomas Lawrence. From 1807 to 1815, the Iron Duke valiantly held the French at bay.

Kitchener moved with his army up the Nile to avenge Gordon's death. In 1898, near Khartoum, Kitchener's army smashed the Mahdists at Omdurman, and the Sudan became an Anglo-Egyptian dependency.

In 1897 Queen Victoria celebrated her Diamond Jubilee on the throne. The British Empire had never been stronger, and stability had come to much of the world. A little island in the North Sea had created a vast colonial realm, a Greater Britain (as the great parliamentarian Charles Dilke hymned it) beyond the seas, a spectacle "unapproached in the whole course of human history." In 1897 one quarter of the surface of the globe was British and one person in five lived under the British flag. The value of exports from the empire had increased four and a half times since Victoria had become queen. The total mileage of imperial railways had increased tenfold; the empire possessed one third of the world's sheep, one fourth of the world's cattle, one twelfth of its horses, one fourteenth of its swine—as well as furnishing one third of the world's gold production.

The last statistic had been substantially increased by the acquisition of the Boer Republics of South Africa through the Boer War of 1899–1902. Complex in origins, the war began in part because Cecil Rhodes had been intent on completing British dominance from the Cape to Cairo, in part because the

At Waterloo (above) on June 18, 1815, Wellington led an eight-hour battle against Napoleon, from which the British and their allies emerged victorious, ending the French challenge forever.

Following pages, a full meeting of the House of Commons, acting as a court and depicted in the fashion of the day, ca. 1820. Each member could be identified by a key that would accompany reprints of the scene for sale to the public.

Boer Republics were now seen to possess great wealth in gold and diamonds, and in part because the Boers, or Dutch Calvinists, themselves had sharply restricted the rights of English-speaking settlers within their republics. Humiliating and costly, the war took 22,000 British, 25,000 Boer, and untold African lives between 1899 and 1902 and cost over 200 million British pounds. A prelude to 1914, the war hinted at the coming decline of the empire.

The British Empire died on the battlefield, losing a generation of leaders in World War One and staggering under the costs of victory in World War Two. In 1928 it was predicted that India would remain within the empire for three hundred years; in 1947 it was independent. In 1952 a Tory leader listed many colo-

149

Above left, the Boston Tea Party, December 1773, at which colonists dressed as Indians dumped tea into Boston harbor. Left, revolutionary batteries at Valley Forge. Below, General George Washington preparing to attack in the battle of Princeton, January 3, 1777.

The American Revolution

"These are the times that try men's souls"—thus wrote Thomas Paine at the end of 1776, as the Americans engaged the vast British empire in the first modern revolution. That revolution ushered in an age of revolutions—French, Greek, broadly European—when people who had once been subservient to another class or nation rose in armed rebellion to declare their independence. The colonists had not wanted war, or even independence, but they felt driven to it by increased British taxation, by limitations on their economic growth and innovation, and by signs that Britain, having vanquished France in war, would now tighten the reins of government. "Those who expect to reap the blessings of freedom must, like men, undergo the fatigue of supporting it," Paine wrote. The same colonists who had loyally fought the French from 1756 to 1763 now turned upon their Mother Country. Refusing to pay military subsidies, then boycotting British goods, the Americans challenged the very idea of a unitary empire. On April 19, 1775—with the celebrated battle of Lexington—the talking stopped and the shooting began.

The American Revolution was "the first modern war" for many reasons, including the skillful use of propaganda by both sides—in these pictures, American. Left, artist John Trumbull's depiction of the Battle of Bunker Hill. Showing the action of June 17, 1775, in which the British dislodged American defenders outside of Boston, the painting was calculated to stir patriotic fervor. So too was the engraving of the Boston Massacre (below left), in which five men were killed.

On July 3, 1776, John Adams, later to become second president of the United States, wrote to his wife, Abigail, that "Yesterday the greatest question was decided which ever was debated in America; and a greater perhaps never was, nor will be, decided among men"—that the colonies would declare themselves independent of Britain, even before they had proved themselves to be. The resolution (below) adopted in committee on July 2 was signed on July 4 and sent to each state legislature.

Artist John Trumbull painted numerous patriotic scenes of the Revolution. His work Signing of the Declaration of Independence (below) was installed in the new Capitol Rotunda in Washington in 1826–1827. Below right, a Gilbert Stuart portrait of George Washington, leader of the rebels and first president of the United States.

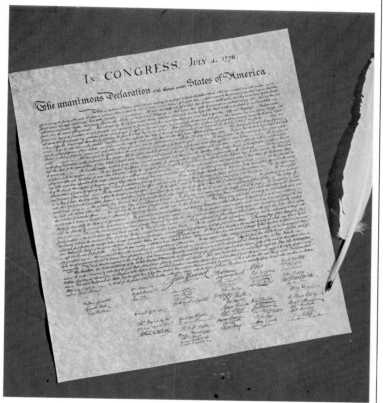

Above, Sir Joshua Reynold's portrait of Warren Hastings, before he became governor-general of India in 1774.

Below, the Government House in Calcutta, India. Before it stands the proud lion, centuries-old symbol of British majesty.

nies for which independence was "inconceivable"; by 1966 all had become new nations.

But the British had left behind more than memories of their rule. They had spread their language, practical arts, and their form of government throughout the world; they had explored it, exploited it, improved it, oppressed it. Until the twentieth century the British Empire had led the world in transportation, communication, sanitation, and education; the British had led the world industrially until the time when Germany and, to an even greater extent, the United States would overtake them.

If they had been imperialists (and they had), few objective observers today could conclude that their imperial rule had not been at least as beneficial to the colonial peoples as that of any other European nation—indeed, more so. The French fablist La Fontaine had written, in 1668, "Those who enjoy power always arrange matters so as to give their tyranny an appearance of justice." Just so, and yet, there had been a sense of justice more readily present in the British Empire—as it became first the *British* Commonwealth of Nations in 1931, and then, in 1947, when it became simply the Commonwealth of Nations—than in most empires at any time. Racism had damaged the image of justice, but the ideal of justice

Above, William IV (reigned 1830–1837). Right, his predecessor George IV, in procession at Westminster. Both were undistinguished monarchs.

had survived. After all, when the Indians, Ceylonese, and Ghanaians demanded independence, it was in the words of the English philosopher Locke, statesman Burke, and prime ministers Disraeli and Gladstone that they did so.

What had it all meant, this greatest of modern empires? Why had it risen, why had it fallen? We are too close to the imperial sunset to answer the last question with any accuracy, for decolonization still continues as tiny lands take their place in the sun: The republic of Kiribati (consisting of the former low-lying coral islands in the Pacific which once bore the name of Thomas Gilbert) is only one of the most recent, following on July 12, 1979, the path taken by its neighboring Ellice Islands, now the republic of

Brighton (above) was the favorite seaside resort of the monarchy. Left, an Indian coin. Right, a political cartoon showing orator and statesman Edmund Burke, Prime Minister North, and liberal, anti-imperialist Charles James Fox attacking Warren Hastings. India had galvanized public interest in the idea of empire as never before.

The hills of England were best conquered by a combination of canals and rail lines. Below, trains bringing coal from the mine at Hetton to a canal by which the cargo was carried to the sea. The English soon dominated railway building and investment throughout the world—in Europe, the Americas, Asia, and Africa. By 1815 canals had brought transport costs down to one third that of road transport; by 1844, railways cost a penny per mile.

Railways

British imperial growth arose partly from technological superiority, especially in modes of transport for heavy goods—and later for troops—on land. The single greatest stride in reducing transport costs and time was the perfection of the iron horse. Many British roads were replaced with parallel rails, first of wood, then of iron, over which a horse could draw a heavily laden cart. These rail-tracks originally operated in conjunction with canals, but once the steam locomotive was developed to overcome the problem of steep gradients, a network of railways stretched throughout Britain. Particularly important to the growth of London, the railroad also made possible the development of the industrial north. On September 27, 1825, George Stephenson initiated the first passenger train, and in 1830 he sent his locomotive, *Rocket*—pulling thirteen tons at an incredible speed of fifteen miles per hour—over the thirty miles from Liverpool to Manchester.

Rails were applied to coal transport in the mines (above) as early as the seventeenth century. By 1804 the steam engine locomotive had been developed by Richard Trevithick, and by 1830 it had been adapted by Stephenson for commercial transportation. Left, a station and tunnel on the Liverpool-Manchester line, opened by Stephenson in 1830. Below, further adaptation to underground traffic.

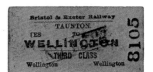

Right, tickets used on English railways and (far right) the London Underground. Below left, an excavation on the famed Liverpool-Manchester line. Below, two views of railway cars and an engine, 1830. Bottom, a viaduct across a canalized river on the Liverpool route.

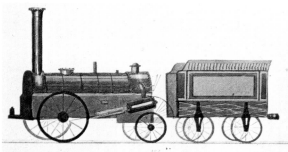

Tuvalu. It has been the duty of another Queen Elizabeth, the Second, to preside over this dissolution of empire—even as small, anomalous reminders of the empire on which the sun never set remain: Gibraltar, Hong Kong, the Falkland Islands, various Caribbean possessions. But why?

There are many answers. Some historians point to a battered Britain, unable to sustain the sinews of an empire after an exhausting world war against Hitler's Germany. Also, after two world wars, the British Empire was simply no longer profitable. Others would point to the United States—perhaps because of its own revolutionary heritage, perhaps because of the rise of its own power—which persistently pressed Britain to free, in particular, its Asian colonies. Others, again, would note how the war in the Pacific, between the United States and Japan during World War Two, inevitably brought Australia, New Zealand, and later Southeast Asia under the American defensive umbrella and away from the British. It was, after all, of the United States that Winston Churchill spoke when he declared, in the midst of the war, that he would not preside over the dissolution of His Majesty's Empire. He did not, though his successors did, following the British and French attempt to retake the Suez Canal in 1956.

After territorial boundaries were redrawn at the Congress of Vienna in 1814–1815, Britain and France drew closer together in their interests, though they continued to compete for an empire in Africa. The early years of Queen Victoria's reign were a period of stability: of friendship with France, as shown by the queen's visit to the French navy (far left) ca. 1840, and of the extension of responsible government to the Canadian colonies in 1841. The young queen, deeply in love with and dependent on her consort, Prince Albert, worked diligently at matters of state—unlike her two immediate predecessors. Queen and consort are shown in a commemorative medal (near left) for the Exhibition of 1851. The exhibition was opened on the banks of the Serpentine, in London's Hyde Park (below left). Especially impressive was the Crystal Palace, designed by Sir Joseph Paxton to provide a showcase for British achievements.

Right, Queen Victoria (reigned 1837–1901) at twenty-three. She and Albert had nine children, and they settled down to a life of middle-class respectability that gave its name to a new puritanism. The queen initially took her cues from Albert, but after his death in 1861, Victoria became a close student of British politics. She liked her Tory prime minister, Benjamin Disraeli, but she was uncomfortable with her Liberal prime minister, William Gladstone, who, she said, always addressed her as though she were a public meeting.

But these reasons, though real, are insufficient, for they omit the other side of the story: the rising surge of nationalism in the colonies themselves. It is patronizing, perhaps even subtly racist, to assume that the history of an empire is solely the history of a European people, for it is, in equal measure, the history of the peoples with whom the Europeans interacted. Nor should one see the impact of imperialism as running in only one direction, as though "native peoples" were always on the receiving end of the benefits—and the blows—of the conquerors. Rather, an empire is a complex meeting of cultures. Today we know it to be condescending to speak of "the natives" as though they did not represent complex societies of their own. We recognize the blindness of the Elizabethans when they referred to the "great vacant lands of the world" which they were to settle—lands not at all vacant, but populated by Red Indians (the British term for the aboriginal population of North America), Maori, Zulu, Luo, Malay, Arawak, or Central Australian aboriginal peoples. These peoples, too, are part of the story of the British Empire, though hardly illustrated here, for their art, politics, social organization, and economies were little recorded by the Europeans.

Then, too, empire and imperialism came to be a

British penetration in Africa

Above left, a map of the Nile basin drawn by British cartographers around 1884. Below, a carved wood panel from the Royal Palace of Ekiti, in southwestern Nigeria. Above right, Scots Highland troops under attack by Fingo tribesmen in September 1851; this incident took place in Natal, *at the height of the so-called Kaffir Wars. Ultimately victorious, the British were then thrust against the Boers—Dutch Calvinist settlers of the Cape Colony in the early 1600s—who had trekked away from the coast to Natal to escape British rule.*

Africa lay on the sea route to the East and was, at first, acquired as a by-product of the imperial desire to control strategic capes and river mouths that dominated the route. In 1441 the Portuguese initiated the overseas export of slaves from western Africa; by 1600 they were supplanted by the Dutch. They in turn were overtaken in the seventeenth century by the British, who in 1663 chartered the Company of Royal Adventurers of England Trading to Africa, establishing slave stations in West Africa. Africa thus best represented the empire of exploitation, as distinct from the empire of settlement. By the 1880s the British and the French were the principal landholders among the contending European powers. In 1919, the British acquired the former German colonies as well: German East Africa (Tanzania), German South-West Africa, Cameroon, and Togo.

Left, a Boer attack on an armored train during the Anglo-Boer War (1899–1902) in the Transvaal. Center, General Charles Gordon, who commanded an Egyptian army against the Mahdiya of the Sudan and was killed in 1885 at Khartoum. In 1896 Lord Kitchener (bottom), the appointed sirdar, or commander, of the Egyptian army, began the reconquest of the Sudan. Henry M. Stanley, the journalist and explorer who was also ruler of the Congo for Leopold of Belgium, and who later won fame by locating the missing missionary-educator David Livingstone, uses the Lady Alice (below) to explore Lake Victoria in East Africa in 1875.

pair of dirty words by the mid-twentieth century. Lord Rosebery, a Liberal, had declared himself proud to be an imperialist, when visiting Australia in 1884. Few would make this boast today, for the word has been appropriated by the political Left as a term of abuse. Even the British people themselves, alert to their own hardships under an oppressive industrial system, had come to recognize in the years after the Boer War that they had contributed to the oppression of others. The opposition to imperialism of some sections of the British working class as well as of certain intellectuals grew stronger in the late nineteenth century; this resulted in changed British attitudes and weakened British resolve to uphold an empire in which the people once took unadulterated pride, but about which they now had increasingly mixed and uneasy feelings.

In the end, decolonization occurred as the colonies learned how to use the technology transferred to them by the West. For ultimately imperialism is, quite simply (and quite complexly), the impact of more highly advanced technological nations on societies of lesser technology. Britain had once possessed a monopoly of technology in its relation to its colonies, and a predominance of technological capacity in relation to its competitors. By 1900 both Germany and the United States had caught up with Britain industrially, and

Top, a crowd at Covent Garden Market, as depicted by Phoebus Levin, an illustrator for Charles Dickens. Above, Derby Day, by William Powell Frith, in 1856. The Derby, begun by the earl of Derby in 1780, is the classic English flat race for three-year-olds, run each year at Epsom, in southern England. The British spread horse racing throughout the empire, opening tracks in Australia, New Zealand, South Africa, and Singapore.

the latter was in a position to deliver its technological capacity to the underdeveloped world equally as well as Britain—especially after the British had lost a generation in the trenches of France during World War One. Those who had chosen to collaborate with the British within the colonies, so that they might be the channels through which the new technology flowed, now were exposed to alternative sources of supply, knowledge, growth, or even of simple hardware. By 1920, Britain had lost, never to regain, its technological lead: The loss of the empire—best accepted through the appearance of a dignified policy of decolonization—was now inevitable.

Why had the empire risen? In part because the British people—that merger of English, Scots, Welsh, and Irish talents—believed in themselves as few nations have done; they were the cutting edge of an advancing Western civilization intent upon reforming—in the original sense of the word, in shaping anew—the world. They needed resources and a predictive capacity over their supply. They sought adventure and knowledge, as well as fields for social and political experimentation.

By the nineteenth century Karl Marx had sought to explain empire, and capitalism, in economic terms; in the twentieth century V. I. Lenin extended his argument. The Marxist-Leninist school of thought held that empires were the highest stage of capitalism before its inevitable decline. Others would mount anti-Marxist arguments, denouncing the limited concept of "economic man." Today more and more of those who seek to "explain" empires hew to neither the Marxist nor the anti-Marxist line, pursuing non-Marxist reasoning that finds, in the infinite complex-

There were, as Disraeli wrote in his novel Sybil, *"two Englands." The fashionable classes often enjoyed private recitals (above right), here painted by the nineteenth-century artist James Tissot. Right, an illustration for Charles Dickens of the poor waiting to be admitted to a hospital. Dickens died in 1870, but his socially realistic novels, especially* Oliver Twist *(1838),* David Copperfield *(1850), and* Hard Times *(1854), influenced social reform long after his death.*

Osborne House

Osborne House was built in 1846 as a summer home for Queen Victoria and her consort, Prince Albert. Near Cowes, on the Isle of Wight, the house was their favorite refuge and a telling showcase of Victoria's taste. Designed by Prince Albert and Thomas Cubitt in the style of a fashionable Italianate villa, the house was furnished in the highly eclectic mode of the times, influenced by the empire. Japanese fans, Turkish hookahs, icons and rosaries, a Malay kris (sword), miniature Indian silver elephants, marble and alabaster statues of historical figures crowded in among the armchairs, stools, poufs, showcases of china, urns, candelabra, picture stands, enameled washstands, flowered carpets, lace curtains, vases of dried flowers under dustproof glass bells, and gas lamps. Clutter and an "artistic impression" were more important than comfort and clean lines.

Dark corridors and low ceilings kept in the heat and created a "cozy" atmosphere in the Gallery of the Marbles (above). Antique and modern figures in the classical mode were exhibited, featuring statues of the Roman nobility as well as works in a sentimental, Victorian vein.

Below left, the entrance to Osborne House, architecturally the high noon of the Victorian Age, set amidst two thousand acres of grounds and gardens. Immediately inside was a hall for a durbar, or Indian-style reception, designed by Rudyard Kipling's father. Victoria kept over four hundred works of art in the house for her aesthetic gratification.

After Albert's death in 1861, the queen, who ever after wore black in mourning, increasingly sought refuge at Osborne, surrounding herself with her cherished possessions. She loved red, which she found soothing, and her reception hall (left) she thought particularly comfortable. From it she could walk quickly to her dining room, where she had affixed a brass plate marking the spot on which Albert lay in state. Above, a view of the gardens from a dressing room window. The grounds included a miniature fort named for Albert, an imported Swiss chalet, and a lifesize doll's house.

Left, a plate commemorating the Golden Jubilee of 1887, which celebrated the fiftieth anniversary of the queen's coronation. Immediately above, a private sitting room at Victoria's preferred retreat. Today Osborne House is open to the public, part as a museum and the remainder as a convalescent home.

Right, Victoria's piano, in the reception hall. Especially popular in the nineteenth century, the piano was necessary even if not played, for it signified a home in which hymns could be sung at daily prayers.

ity of human action, myriad explanations, overlapping and intertwined, to account for why one nation came to dominate so much of the globe.

They note that the British Empire, in particular, grew with the active cooperation of the elite among the Indians, the Fijians, the Egyptians, the Greeks, the Maori, and the Africans, who for reasons of their own chose to collaborate toward a common end: improved trade and various forms of modernization. When Disraeli purchased the French shares to the Suez Canal, he did so with the blessings of the Egyptians. When he went to the Berlin Congress, he received the eager cooperation of the Turkish, or Ottoman, throne, which also sought to limit Russian expansion in the Near East. When Lord Aberdeen and Lord Rosebery sat down to dine, they spoke together of the Great Game—of the contest with Russia for dominance of the Northwest Frontier of India—as precisely that, fun and exciting, as well as important. For the empire grew over the course of many little wars, none of which could have—as today any war

might do—destroyed the world. The empire grew in an era of confidence.

That confidence remains stamped upon the globe. The very geography of the world as we know it is the product of the European empire: Near East, Middle East, Far East. Such regions are near, middle, and far only in relation to a geography determined by those isles set in a silver sea. Even our sense of time is the product of the British Empire, for Greenwich Mean Time, set just above the south bank of the Thames River, determines the time for the peoples of the world. The imperial revolution, led by the British, has changed the world; and yet we are still in the midst of that revolution. In the end Britain lost its possessions but it did not give up its influence, engraved on our mental maps, embedded in our language, ticking within our mental timepieces.

Who has not read the romantic novelists of the empire—G. A. Henty, H. Rider Haggard, Rudyard Kipling? Who does not know *Kim* or *The Jungle Book*? Who has not experienced the thrill of spy and detec-

The British became enveloped in memories of their empire. Above, the slaughterhouse in Cawnpore, unhappy reminder of the Indian Mutiny. Below left, Disraeli meeting with a representative of Turkey at the Berlin Congress of 1878. Below right, Lord Rosebery, father of the phrase "Commonwealth of Nations," dining with fellow Liberals. Victoria (right) appears to oversee all.

tive fiction, and yet perhaps not recognized their imperial overtones: Sherlock Holmes' companion, Dr. Watson, just back from Afghanistan; John Buchan's Richard Hannay learning the tricks by which he foils the enemies of the empire while in southern Africa. Even Ian Fleming's James Bond learned that his martinis must be shaken and not stirred while in Jamaica. Winnie-the-Pooh and Beatrix Potter's Peter Rabbit, the great figures of comic humor and boyhood adventure, from Robinson Crusoe through Long John Silver to even William Golding's *Lord of the Flies*—all carry their readers subtly, largely unconsciously, into the empire of the British. As an empire of the mind, it will long be with us.

The British Empire of fact, like all empires, proved to be transient. The Romans had erected buildings on the Isle of Wight off the southern coast of England; later the British would wed their castles to Roman forts, would preserve the remnants of the great empire that had preceded theirs as reminders of their own antiquity, as harbingers of their own decline. This is the Ozymandias principle, of which British radical Percy Bysshe Shelley wrote so movingly in 1817:

> I met a traveler from an antique land
> Who said: "Two vast and trunkless legs of stone
> Stand in the desert. . . Near them, on the sand,
> Half sunk, a shattered visage lies, whose frown,
> And wrinkled lip, and sneer of cold command,
> Tell that its sculptor well those passions read
> Which yet survive, stamped on these lifeless things,
> The hand that mocked them, and the heart that fed:
> And on the pedestal these words appear:
> "My name is Ozymandias, King of Kings:
> Look on my works, ye Mighty and despair!"
> Nothing beside remains. Round the decay
> Of that colossal wreck, boundless and bare
> The lone and level sands stretch far away.

The hand belonged to the sculptor, the heart to the king, nursing the passions the sculptor read. Today the hand belongs to the historian who must account for so great an empire in its glory—and for its passions spent. To tread on an empire's dust, as Shelley's contemporary Lord Byron remarked, is to be reminded of the earthquake that was once below.

Photography Credits

Arborio Mella: p. 24, p. 29 bottom right, p. 31 bottom right, p. 44 left, p. 50 top left, pp. 50–51 bottom / *Berengo-Gardin:* p. 11 top and bottom, p. 12 right, p. 90 top left / *Bodleian Library:* p. 107 bottom right / *Bristol Record Office:* p. 102 bottom left / *British Museum:* p. 92, p. 99 bottom right, p. 101, p. 106 top, p. 107 top right, p. 154 bottom, p. 155 bottom right / *Bulloz:* p. 74 / *J. Allan Cash:* pp. 90–91 center, p. 91 top right, p. 99 top right / *Cauchetier:* p. 25 left, p. 43 bottom left, p. 63 bottom right / *Cooper-Bridgeman Library:* p. 99 left, p. 146 bottom / *Costa:* p. 9, p. 10 bottom, p. 20 bottom, p. 21 top right, p. 34 bottom left and right, p. 81 bottom right, p. 83 bottom right, p. 93 top, p. 104 top, p. 114 bottom right, p. 148 bottom left, p. 155 bottom left, p. 156 bottom left and right, p. 157 center left and bottom, p. 167 bottom left / *Dulevant:* p. 45 right, p. 66 top left / *M. Evans Picture Library:* p. 126 bottom / *W. Forman:* p. 99 center right, p. 100 right, p. 160 bottom / *Foto Atélier:* p. 105 / *Freeman:* p.119 bottom right / *Giraudon:* p. 26 bottom, pp. 60–61, p. 68 bottom left, p. 70 top 4th from left & center 2nd from left, p. 81 top right and bottom center / *Giraudon-CLF:* p. 68 bottom right / *Giraudon-Lauros:* p. 66 center, p. 67 top and bottom, p. 78 top left, p. 80 bottom / *R. Harding:* p. 117 top right and bottom, pp. 118–119 center, pp. 122–123 top, p. 156 top and center, p. 158 top right, p. 162, p. 163, p. 166 right, p. 167 bottom right / *Hornak:* p. 89, p. 93 bottom, p. 96 left, p. 100 bottom left, p. 106 bottom, pp. 106–107 center, p. 118 center left / *London, Wellington Museum:* p. 149 / *Kunsthistorisches Museum, Vienna:* p. 108 top 1st from left / *Magnum-Burri:* p. 36 top / *Magnum-Freed:* p. 13 top / *Magnum-Hartmann:* p. 97 right / *Magnum-Lessing:* p. 16 top left and bottom left, p. 17 top right, p. 36 bottom right, p. 48 bottom left, p. 98 left, p. 139 bottom, p. 164, p. 165 / *Magnum-Rodger:* p. 54 bottom right, p. 109 center right / *Mairani:* p. 23 bottom left, p. 28 right, p. 32 bottom, p. 63 top right, p. 68 top right, p. 69 top, p. 75 top left, p. 76 top right, p. 84 center left, p. 91 top left, p. 97 top left, p. 118 bottom left and right, p. 119 bottom left, p. 124 bottom left, p. 129 bottom, p. 143 bottom, p. 152 bottom left / *Marka:* p. 10 top / *Marka-Everts:* p. 35 bottom / *The Museum of London:* p. 127 right, pp. 130–131, p. 137 top, p. 144 bottom left, p. 155 top right, p. 158 bottom / *National Portrait Gallery, London:* p. 108 top 2nd from left, p. 108 top 4th from left, p. 111 top and bottom center, p. 133 right bottom and top, pp. 150–151 top / *National Trust, England:* p. 143 top / *OPI:* p. 11 center, p. 12 bottom left, pp. 20–21 top center, p. 21 bottom left, p. 27 top, p. 31 bottom left, p. 38 top, p. 49 bottom right, p. 58 top, bottom left and right / *Paris, Bibliothèque Nationale:* p. 15 center left / *Pellegrini:* p. 90 center right / *Photri:* p. 152 top left and bottom right, pp. 152–153 center top, p. 153 bottom left / *Publifoto:* p. 13 bottom / *Pucciarelli:* pp. 18–19, p. 30 top, p. 31 top left and right, p. 38 bottom, p. 52 left, p. 57 top, p. 64 top right, p. 83 bottom left, p. 84 bottom left, pp. 84–85 bottom center, p. 86 bottom, p. 96 right, p. 97 bottom left, p. 102 top left, p. 109 top and bottom right, p. 111 right center and bottom right, p. 115, p. 123 bottom 4th from left, p. 124 bottom right, p. 127 left, p. 128 bottom right, p. 144 bottom right, p. 167 top / *Ricciarini-Arch. B:* p. 14 bottom, p. 15 top right and center right, p. 26 top, pp. 46–47, p. 64 bottom left, p. 66 bottom left, p. 70 top 2nd from left, p. 78 top right, p. 84 top left, pp. 84–85 top center, p. 85 bottom right, p. 123 bottom 1st from left, p. 137 bottom, p. 142 top right / *Ricciarini-Simion:* p. 30 bottom left, p. 31 center right, p. 37 top left, p. 43 top and bottom right, pp. 62–63 bottom center, p. 75 center right and bottom, p. 76 top left, p. 78 bottom left, p. 119 top, p. 138 bottom left, p. 146 top right, p. 166 left / *Ricciarini-Tomsich:* p. 39 left, p. 51 right, p. 103, p. 114 top right, p. 120, p. 121 top and bottom right, p. 122 bottom, p. 123 bottom 2nd from left, p. 124 top, p. 128 left, p. 144 top left / *Ricciarini-Unedi:* p. 14 top, p. 15 bottom right, bottom left and center, p. 16 right, p. 22 left, p. 23 top and bottom right, p. 28 left, p. 29 top right, p. 32 top, p. 33, p. 37 bottom, pp. 44–45 bottom center, p. 49 left and right top, p. 52 right / *Lares Riva:* p. 22 right, p. 39 right, p. 100 top left, p. 114 left, p. 121 bottom left / *Rizzoli:* p. 21 bottom right, p. 34 top left, p. 35 top, p. 48 right, p. 54 top left, p. 55 bottom, p. 57 bottom, p. 58 top left, p. 59, p. 64 top left, p. 65, p. 68 top left, p. 70 top 1st from left, center 1st from left, center 3rd from left, and bottom all pictures, p. 72 top, p. 76 bottom, p. 77, p. 78 bottom right, p. 79, p. 81 top left and bottom left, p. 83 top right, p. 86 top, p. 94 center, p. 95, p. 98 top right and bottom, p. 109 bottom left, pp. 116–117 top center, p. 118 top left, p. 123 bottom 3rd from left, p. 125, p. 126 top, p. 128 top right, p. 129 top, p. 132 left and right, pp. 134–135, p. 136, p. 138 top and center, bottom center and right, p. 139 top, p. 140, p. 142 top left and bottom, p. 144 top right, p. 145, p. 146 top left, p. 147, p. 148 top and bottom right, p. 157 top and center right, p. 158 top left, p. 160 top left and right, p. 161 left center and bottom / *Scala:* p. 108 bottom / *SEF:* p. 53 bottom, p. 66 bottom right and top right, p. 67 center, p. 69 bottom, p. 70 3rd from left, p. 80 top, p. 153 center left, top right, and bottom right, p. 161 top, p. 167 center / *Titus:* p. 15 top left, p. 20 top center, p. 25 right, p. 29 left, p. 30 bottom right, p. 36 center and bottom left, p. 37 top right, p. 42, pp. 44–45 top center, p. 48 left, p. 50 top right, p. 53 top, p. 54 top right and bottom left, p. 56, p. 71, p. 72 bottom, p. 73, p. 75 top, p. 82, p. 83 top left and bottom center, p. 87, p. 90 center left, p. 91 bottom, p. 94 top and bottom, p. 107 top left, p. 110, p. 116 bottom, p. 141 top right, p. 155 top left, p. 159, p. 161 bottom right / *Titus-Beaujard:* p. 12 top left, p. 62 top left and bottom, pp. 62–63 top center / *E. Tweedy:* p. 104 bottom / *V. & A. Museum, London:* p. 102 top right and bottom / *J. Webb:* p. 155 center / *Woburn Abbey, England:* p. 108 top 3rd from left /

Index